PUNCTUATION:
The Ultimate Guide

GIACOMO GIAMMATTEO

Inferno Publishing Company

© **2017** Giacomo Giammatteo. All rights reserved. No part of this book may be reproduced or transmitted in any form or by any means, electronic or mechanical, including photocopying, recording, or by any information storage and retrieval system, without written permission from the author, except for the inclusion of brief quotations in a review.

Inferno Publishing Company

Houston, TX

For more information about this book, visit my website.

Edition ISBNs

Trade Paperback ......

E-book 978-1-949074-54-3

Cover design by Natasha Brown

Book design by Giacomo Giammatteo

This edition was prepared by Giacomo Giammatteo gg@giacomog.com

✽ Created with Vellum

INTRODUCTION

Grammar consists of many things, and one of the more important is punctuation. It is like the Rosetta Stone, providing the key to how writers want a reader to interpret what they wrote.

Punctuation is even present when we speak. A slight pause is similar to a comma, a longer pause akin to a semicolon, and a stop equals a period. Question marks and exclamation points can be heard in the cadence of a person's speech pattern and where the emphasis is placed and on which words.

Almost all punctuation marks are represented in everyday speech, and therein lies the key to great dialogue—knowing how to use punctuation correctly with dialogue.

There are some writers who are masters at it. Elmore Leonard was one of the best. Read his books, or listen to a few of the movies made from his books, and you'll see a genius's work.

This book explains how to use punctuation in an easy-to-grasp manner.

Part One
PUNCTUATION

It's been said before, but it's worth repeating: punctuation is like a traffic system. Each punctuation mark tells the reader what to do: stop as if it were a red light (period); slow down similar to a yellow light (comma); or pause like a yield sign (semicolon). Other marks carry different messages. (Depending on how you drive, the comma and semicolon signals may be reversed.)

The thing to remember is that without punctuation, readers have no way of knowing what the writer intends.

Without further ado, let's dig into the sometimes-confusing world of punctuation.

I always say my books will not venture into using grammatical terms, but punctuation requires a little more than most. Still, it won't get too technical. I promise.

One more thing before we move on.

Many of the online grammar sites and even the style guides and dictionaries I checked refer to a lot of rules using the terms *always* or *never*, when what they should say is *usually* or *seldom*.

Always means "on every occasion" or "all the time."

Never means "not at any time" or "at no time."

If a rule has exceptions (and most do), then you shouldn't use *always* or *never*.

A couple of examples of what I'm speaking of are below, and they deal with the use of punctuation used with quotation marks.

More than one site said, "Periods and commas *never* go outside quotation marks" and "All other punctuation *always* goes outside quotation marks." As you'll see in the "Quotation Marks" chapter, that isn't *always* the case.

Part One
COMMAS

A couple of these examples were taken from a *Business Insider* article and a couple were taken from the Grammarly site; the rest are mine.

Commas are one of the worst offenders when it comes to misuse. Many writers think they can do whatever they want with a comma and no one will be the wiser, nor will the reader question them. A mistake or misplaced comma can be chalked up to a writer's style, they say.

But nothing is further from the truth. When it comes to commas, there are strict guidelines on when to use them and when not to use them. It's true that you can get away with a few misuses and attribute it to a stylistic choice, but too many mistakes will draw the critics out in droves.

I break one of the comma rules when writing dialogue in my novels, but it's a subtle misuse, and most people probably don't even notice. I do it because I think the book reads better that way. But the remainder of rules regarding punctuation I adhere to, or at least I try to.

Chapter One
COMMA RULES

One note about commas before we begin. Commas are meant to indicate a pause or a break between the different parts of a sentence. Above all else, they are meant to clarify or make the meaning more clear. They do this in various ways: to separate items in a list, to offset the nonessential parts of a sentence, to mark a pause following an introductory clause or word, and to note who is being spoken to when using dialogue.

The main thing to understand is that commas are not there because of some arbitrary rule; the rules regarding when and how to use commas exist to enhance clarity—no other reason.

With that said, let's delve into the rules on commas.

Rule 1

- Use a comma after a dependent clause that starts a sentence.

I told you I wouldn't resort to grammatical terms, so let's dumb it down. A "dependent clause" is no different than a dependent child; they both rely on something else for support. A dependent child relies on their parents or guardians, and a dependent clause relies on the rest of the sentence for support; in other words, it doesn't make sense by itself. Let's look at a few examples:

- When I went to the bank, (dependent clause).
- When I took a walk, (dependent clause).
- After driving to the city, (dependent clause).

All the above are dependent clauses and require more substance to complete the sentence. Examples are below:

- When I went to the bank, I made a deposit (complete sentence).
- When I took a walk, I got robbed (complete sentence).
- After driving to the city, I lay down and napped (complete sentence).

If you switch the order of the sentence, the comma is no longer needed. Let's take a look.

- I made a deposit when I went to the bank.
- I got robbed when I took a walk.
- I lay down for a nap after driving to the city.

That took a lot of explaining for one simple rule, but I like to use examples because I think people understand them better.

Rule 2

- Use a comma before a coordinating conjunction that connects two independent clauses.

That rule is rife with grammatical terms, so let's break it down in plain English.

A "coordinating conjunction" is a word that *connects*. In this case, it connects two "independent clauses," which means they could be stand-alone sentences. Let's look at a few examples.

PS: from now on, when I refer to a "connecting word," it means a conjunction of some sort; after all, a *conjunction connects.*

✅ I went to the bank, and I made a deposit.

✅ I took a walk, and I got robbed.

In both of the sentences above, each part of the sentence on either side of the connecting word *and* could be its own sentence.

- I went to the bank.
- I made a deposit.

If you remove the subject (I) from the second part, though, it changes everything because that sentence can no longer stand on its own, which means you no longer need a comma to separate them.

✅ I went to the bank and made a deposit.

✅ I took a walk and got robbed.

The coordinating conjunctions (connecting words) are easy to remember if you use the acronym, FANBOYS. It stands for: *for, and, nor, but, or, yet,* and *so.*

There are other types of conjunctions (or connecting words), but we'll get to them at another time.

Rule 3

- Use a comma to separate items in a list of three or more.

This rule applies when you have three or more items. In the following sentence only two items are mentioned, so you don't need a comma to separate them.

❌ I went to the bank to make a deposit, and get a withdrawal (two items).

✅ I went to the bank to make a deposit, get a withdrawal, and open a new account (three items).

❌ The sandwiches I like are turkey, and peanut butter.

✅ The sandwiches I like are turkey, peanut butter, and tomato with cheese.

You need to be careful when using commas with lists. There is still a controversy regarding the use of the final comma, which is referred to as the Oxford comma. Some people swear by it, while others claim it is not needed.

The Oxford comma is suggested for a reason: to clear up ambiguity. Take the last sentence and look at it both ways.

✅ The sandwiches I like are turkey, peanut butter, and tomato with cheese.

❌ The sandwiches I like are turkey, peanut butter and tomato with cheese.

Although I doubt this would confuse anyone, it could. Taken at face value, the sentence could mean that you like turkey sandwiches as well as peanut-butter-and-tomato sandwiches with cheese.

I am a proponent of the Oxford comma, and if you want to be understood clearly, I suggest you follow suit.

I'll give one more example. One of my favorite movies is an older western featuring Clint Eastwood. The title is: *The Good, the Bad and the Ugly*. And it's punctuated exactly that way, with no comma after *bad*.

However, when I say it, and when I hear others pronounce the name, there is a definite pause after *bad* as if a comma belongs there. In fact, the Italian name for the movie (it was made in Italy) is *Il Buono, il Brutto, il Cattivo*.

As you can see, there are commas after all the nouns. I think it sounds better that way.

Besides, if you don't use a comma, it could be interpreted as being about two people: the good, and the bad and ugly. With the comma, it leaves no doubt: the good, the bad, and the ugly.

Rule 4

- Use a comma to offset nonessential information.

I'll simplify this. If you have a phrase or part of a sentence that is merely there to provide additional information, use a comma to offset it.

Use a comma before it if it completes the sentence, and on each side of it if it comes in the middle of the sentence. Examples follow:

☑ I went to the bank and saw Jane, one of the tellers.

☑ I went to the bank and saw Jane, one of the tellers, as she got out of the cab.

In each case, the phrase offset by the comma was not needed.

☑ I went to the bank and saw Jane.

☑ I went to the bank and saw Jane as she got out of the cab.

As you can see, when we removed "one of the tellers" from each sentence, it was still a complete sentence and the meaning didn't change. "One of the tellers" was simply additional information about Jane.

If the word or phrase is necessary though, *do not* use a comma. Here are a couple of sentences showing the difference.

☑ My niece Bella calls me almost every night.

☑ My wife, Mikki, fixes my coffee every day.

In the first sentence, we didn't use a comma because *Bella* is a necessary part of the sentence. I needed to mention her name to distinguish her from the other nieces I have. If I had just said, "My niece calls me almost every night" you wouldn't know which niece calls.

In the second sentence, however, *Mikki* is not needed because I only have one wife. There is no need to mention her name.

Rule 5

Use a comma to offset a negative comment in opposition to the sentence. And use it whether it occurs mid-sentence or at the end.

- I went to the bank, not the restaurant.
- I stopped at the restaurant, not the bank, so I have no money.

Rule 6

Place a comma between adjectives that modify the same noun. It will be easier to show this with examples.

- Mollie was a pretty mean dog.
- The bear that attacked was a big, furry bear.
- She lived in a big, expensive house.

Sometimes several adjectives are used before a noun but don't modify the noun the same way. If they modify the noun independently, put a comma between them.

There are several ways you can tell whether to use a comma or not. The first is to place the word *and* between the adjectives and see if the sentence still makes sense. Let's take the sentences above and check.

- Mollie was a pretty and mean dog.
- The bear that attacked was a big *and* furry bear.
- She lived in a big *and* expensive house.

Sentence number one changes meaning. Mollie goes from being considered "pretty mean" (somewhat mean) to being thought of as *pretty* and *mean*.

Sentences two and three sound fine. "It was a big and furry bear" and "She lived in a big and expensive house." Neither of those sentences are ideal as far as I'm concerned, but they work.

The second way to determine what and how the adjectives modify is to rearrange them.

- Mollie was a mean pretty dog.
- The bear that attacked was a furry, big bear.
- She lived in an expensive, big house.

Now look at each sentence, and how rearranging the adjectives affected the meaning. In sentence one, it now reads "Mollie was a mean pretty dog," meaning Mollie was a pretty dog that was mean. That's different than the original. In the original, it said Mollie was mean, but it didn't imply she was pretty.

Sentences two and three don't change in meaning.

Rule 7

- When a title follows a name, use commas to separate it from the rest of the sentence.

Again, examples show it best.

- Donald Trump, the president, is disliked by many people.
- Sean McGonnigle, the chief of police, was reappointed by the mayor.

Rule 8

- Use commas to separate the month and day from the year in a date, and to separate the street address, city, and state in an address.

As usual, examples follow:

- He was born on April 21, 2015.
- He lives at 555 Orange Street, Austin, TX 78617.

If only the month and year are used, no comma is necessary.

- He was born in April 2015

Rule 9

- Use commas to separate numbers of four digits or more.

Most everyone knows this, but we'll give examples just in case.

- 36,577
- 1,998

- 124,222
- 2,467,655

One more note about commas with numbers:

If you are writing about metric measurements, use spaces instead of commas. This will avoid confusion for European readers who are accustomed to seeing commas used as decimal points. The examples below will show it better.

- He bought a farm in Tuscany, a 16,7 hectare one (European way).
- He bought a farm in Tuscany, a 16.7 hectare one (U.S. way).
- For the resort, they needed a minimum of 2 449 hectares. (A space was used instead of a comma.)

If we had used a comma and not a space in the last example, a person used to seeing commas used as decimal points would have read that as "2.449" hectares (quite a difference).

Rule 10

- Use a comma after an adverb that introduces a clause.

Here are a few example sentences:

- Inadvertently, I spilled the wine.
- Finally, he caught the killer.
- Mistakenly, he locked her up.

Many guides make exceptions for one-word introductions where clarity is not affected. The words *now, nowadays, today,* and *yesterday* are some of the words allowed exceptions.

- Yesterday we went to the zoo.

You *could* use a comma after *yesterday*, but you don't have to. Either way is fine. The following sentences are more examples:

- Now is the time to go.
- Nowadays everyone has a cell phone.

Rule 11

- Use a comma *after* a conjunctive (connecting) adverb that links/connects two independent clauses.

Below are examples:

- My sister got carded at the store; therefore, we got no wine.
- My dog isn't very big; however, he scared off the intruder.
- She studied hard for the test; consequently, she got an *A*.

If the situation does not call for a semicolon, use commas on either side of the conjunctive adverb (connecting word).

- He didn't believe, however, that money was a factor.

Below is a list to use as a reference.

LIST OF CONJUNCTIVE ADVERBS

- accordingly
- additionally
- also
- besides
- comparatively
- consequently

- conversely
- elsewhere
- equally
- finally
- further
- furthermore
- hence
- henceforth
- however
- in addition
- in comparison
- in contrast
- indeed
- instead
- likewise
- meanwhile
- moreover
- namely
- nevertheless
- next
- nonetheless
- now
- otherwise
- rather
- similarly
- still
- subsequently
- then
- thereafter
- therefore
- thus.
- yet

Rule 12

- Use commas when attributing quotes.

Whether you're writing novels or nonfiction, you will invariably come across the need to use a direct quote, and when you do, a comma will be needed to offset that quote. The examples below show how.

- "I'm not staying," Joe said. "I'll be leaving after dinner."
- Margaret glared and said, "Why not?"

Rule 13

- Use a comma after *yes* and *no* when they occur at the beginning of a sentence.

Take a look at the two examples below:

- *Yes*, I'm going to the bank.
- *No*, I won't be making a deposit while I'm there.

Rule 14

Use a comma when directly addressing someone.

- It's time for us to go, Captain.
- You'll go, Detective, when I say you can go.
- Captain, it's not right to hold us back.

This doesn't cover every instance where you may need a comma, but it covers most of them. Even a professional writer may go years without encountering a circumstance not mentioned here.

At the end of the next chapter, we cover many examples of how and when to use commas with specific words and phrases.

Part One
MORE COMMA RULES

Like everything else, there are rules that govern punctuation with dialogue tags. It just so happens that one of them I don't agree with.

There aren't many times when I don't listen to my editors, but there are a few. I don't mean the odd occurrence when an editor may make a call on whether to capitalize a word or something like that. I'm talking about repeated usage that is contrary to the *rules* of writing.

I'm going to discuss one of those rules now. It deals with the use of commas. But before we do that, let's take a look at some other rules governing comma usage.

I know we just spent a lot of time learning about commas, but they're tricky to understand, so it may be worthwhile to review some of the rules. If you don't think you need to go over them, skip this part.

What Are Commas Used For?

According to the *Oxford English Dictionary*:

A comma marks a slight break between different parts of a sentence. Used properly, commas make the meaning of sentences clear by grouping and separating words, phrases, and clauses. Many people are uncertain about the use of commas and often sprinkle them throughout their writing without knowing the basic rules.

Here are the main cases when you need to use a comma:
- in lists of three or more items
- in direct speech
- to separate clauses
- to set off certain parts of a sentence
- with *however* and other conjunctions (connecting words)

There are a lot of rules governing the use of commas, and some of them can be confusing. The rules dealing with lists and dialogue are fairly rigid, but they are also simple to understand. The separation of clauses is more complex. I've tried to list the more confusing ones below, and I explain them in plain language instead of using grammatical terms so that anyone can understand how it's done.

I sometimes think that dictionaries and grammarians are associated with the legal and insurance professions; they continually try to complicate things with obscure language.

WHEN NOT TO USE COMMAS

There are a few hard-and-fast rules, and there's one I see broken frequently. I'm guilty of it myself. What rule?

Do *not* use commas *after* "such as, like, or although"—unless what follows is a nonessential clause (unnecessary).

Examples follow:

✗ I love Italian foods such as, ravioli, lasagna, and gnocchi.

✓ I love Italian foods, such as ravioli, lasagna, and gnocchi.

✓ I love Italian foods, such as ravioli, lasagna, and gnocchi, but not dishes that include seafood.

Commas are required when the clause is not needed for the sentence to be true. Take the clause out and see: "I love Italian foods but not dishes that include seafood."

The next few examples deal with using commas with the word *although* and *like*.

❌ I like Italian food although, I eat steaks every week (no comma *after although*).

✅ I like Italian food, although I eat steaks every week.

❌ Even though I love Italian food, I eat things like, burgers and hot dogs (no comma after *like*).

✅ Even though I love Italian food, I eat things like burgers and hot dogs.

Do not use commas in front of dependent words, like *because, when, if, until, and unless*. (For a more complete list of dependent words, see the list on my website.)

❌ The dog was panting, because it had just chased the mailman.

✅ The dog was panting because it had just chased the mailman.

❌ We'll go to the mall, when your mother gets home.

✅ We'll go to the mall when your mother gets home.

When to Use a Comma

Use a comma after a dependent clause that starts a sentence.

- "When I went to the bank, I made a deposit."

As mentioned previously, a dependent clause cannot stand on its own. It is not a complete sentence, and that's why it's called a dependent clause; it needs the rest of the sentence to support it.

Commas always follow these clauses when they're found at the start of a sentence, but when a dependent clause ends the sentence, it no longer requires a comma:

- "I went to the bank and made a deposit"
- "I made a deposit when I went to the bank."

Use commas to separate independent clauses when they are joined by any of these seven coordinating conjunctions: *and, but, for, or, nor, so, yet.*

☑ "I went to the bank *and* made a deposit." (No comma before *and* because "made a deposit" is not a complete sentence.)

☑ I went to the bank, *and* I made a deposit. A comma is necessary because "I made a deposit" is a complete sentence.

✗ I went to the bank, *and* made a deposit. (No comma is necessary.)

✗ I went to the bank *and* I made a deposit. (Comma is necessary after *bank*.)

And don't forget that the comma goes *before* the conjunction (for, and, nor, but, or, yet, so), not *after* it.

There is a case where a comma also goes after the connecting word. Look at the following, which you'll see later as well.

- A semicolon should not be used in place of a colon. It's not a good substitute, and, despite its name association, it doesn't want to be a colon.

Notice the comma after *and*. We need a comma there because the phrase that follows—despite its name association—is a nonessential clause; it's not needed. Take it out and see.

- A semicolon should not be used in place of a colon. It's not a good substitute, and it doesn't want to be a colon.

As you can see, we still need the comma preceding *and* because it joins two independent clauses.

Note: Many style guides (and editors) might recommend omitting the comma after 'and' since the trend is to eliminate punctuation when possible but technically it's correct.

Dependent markers are words added to the beginning of an independent clause that make it a dependent clause. The following is a list of those words:

- **after**
- **although**
- **as**
- **as if**
- **because**
- **before**
- **even if**
- **even though**
- **if**
- **in order to**
- **since**
- **though**
- **unless**
- **until**
- **whatever**
- **when**
- **whenever**
- **whether**
- **while**

An example might be:

- I made a deposit *when* I went to the bank.

Notice that "I made a deposit" and "I went to the bank" are both independent clauses, but by adding *when* to the beginning of the second clause, it becomes a dependent clause because you didn't just make a deposit, you made it *when you went to the bank*.

Another example could be shown by turning the sentence around.

- When I went to the bank, I made a deposit.

Note that we need a comma after bank in this situation because it falls under the rule mentioned earlier: use a comma after a dependent clause that starts a sentence.

Now we're about to get confusing, so put on your learner's hat.

Independent Marker Word

An independent marker word is a connecting word used at the beginning of an independent clause. These words can always begin a complete sentence.

When the second independent clause in a sentence has an independent marker word, a semicolon is needed before the independent marker word (yes, that dreaded semicolon). These words are also called *conjunctive adverbs*.

☑ I wasn't planning on going to the bank; *however*, I needed to make a deposit.

As you can see *however* joins the two independent clauses using a semicolon.

☑ I don't want to go to the bank; *nevertheless*, I need to make a deposit.

☑ "I'll be driving down Fourth Street; *therefore*, I'll stop by the bank and make a deposit.

A Partial List of Independent Marker Words/Conjunctive Adverbs

- also
- consequently
- fortunately
- furthermore
- hopefully
- however
- in addition
- in fact
- instead
- likewise
- meanwhile
- moreover
- nevertheless

- on the other hand
- otherwise
- therefore
- unfortunately

There are other words that could be added to this list, but these are the more commonly used ones.

Use commas before every sequence of three numbers when writing a number larger than 999. (Two exceptions are when writing years and house numbers.)

For example, you would write numbers this way: 4,176 or 10,000 or 1,304,687.

But you would write, "He was born in 1972," and "She lives at 2419 Canal Street."

Use commas before and after nonessential words, phrases, and clauses—that is, parts of the sentence that interrupt it without changing the essential meaning.

Below is an example of such a sentence. It's a sentence I used previously, but it's a good example.

☑ A semicolon should not be used in place of a colon. It's not a good substitute, and, despite its name association, it doesn't want to be a colon.

Note that this breaks the *rule* that says *not* to place a comma *after* a coordinating conjunction, but an analysis will show that the comma after *substitute* is required because it separates two independent clauses, and the comma after *and* is required because it precedes a nonessential phrase ("despite its name association"). That phrase is nonessential because if you remove it, the sentence still makes sense and the meaning doesn't change.

☑ A semicolon should not be used in place of a colon. It's not a good substitute, and it doesn't want to be a colon.

With the preceding sentence, you can eliminate that comma by rewording the sentence to make the second clause dependent:

☑ A semicolon should not be used in place of a colon. It's not a good substitute and doesn't want to be a colon.

Below are a few examples of combining appositives with nonessential phrases.

☑ My wife, Mikki, who loves to shop, is at the fabric store.

☑ My brother Chris, who loves to drink, is at the store getting beer.

In the first example, we used commas to offset *Mikki*, as it is nonessential. Since I only have one wife, naming Mikki is unnecessary. We also offset the nonessential phrase "who loves to shop," as it is not necessary. As you can see below, the sentence works fine without either one of these.

☑ My wife is at the fabric store.

In the second example, we don't offset *Chris* with commas as I have more than one brother, so using his name is necessary. The nonessential phrase follows the same reasoning as the first example. Now look at the essential parts of that sentence.

☑ My brother Chris is at the store getting beer.

There is a time (when using a nonessential clause) that you should opt for a different punctuation mark. I cover this later on in the chapter dealing with dashes, but it won't hurt to touch on it here.

We've gone over nonessential phrases and how you should use commas to offset them, but there is an exception. (Isn't there always?)

If that *additional* bit of information contains commas of its own, use an *em dash* on either side of it instead of a comma; it makes it easier to understand. I've included an example of that below, where the sentence is presented both ways—with and without the em dash.

- My van, the one with the wheelchair ramp, automatic doors, and wench, is black.

- My van—the one with the wheelchair ramp, automatic doors, and wench—is black.

As you can see, the use of the em dashes makes the sentence easier to read than the one without em dashes.

Use commas to separate items in a series of three or more:

- My brother Chris picked up hot dogs, hamburgers, potato chips, and Coke when he went to the store.

If he had only picked up two items, the commas would not have been necessary.

- My brother Chris picked up hot dogs and hamburgers when he went to the store.

And notice in the first example, there is no comma following *Coke* and before *went*. You only use commas to separate the items in the list.

Use a comma after introductory adverbs.

☑ Finally, he got home with the food.
☑ At last, I could breathe.

Also insert a comma when phrases like "on the other hand," *however*, and *furthermore* start a sentence.

No comma is necessary with *however* when it is used to mean "no matter how" or "to whatever extent."

- *However* you do it, get it done.
- *However* it has to be done, just do it.

Look at the sentences with those meanings substituted.

- No matter how you do it, get it done.
- Whatever has to be done, just do it.

Use a comma when attributing quotes.

The rule for where the comma goes depends on where the attribution is placed within the sentence.

If attribution comes before the quote, place the comma prior to and outside of the quotations marks:

- My brother said, "I picked up some beer."

But if the attribution comes after the quote, put the comma inside the closing quotation marks.

- "I got some beer," said my brother (or "my brother said").

Use a comma to separate each element in an address. Also use a comma after a city-state combination within a sentence.

☑ I work downtown at 1212 Milam Street, Houston, Texas 77070.

or

☑ I love to visit San Francisco, California, one of my favorite cities.

Use commas to separate full dates (weekday, month and day, and year). Separate the parts of an address from each other as well as from the rest of the sentence.

☑ August 1, 1960, was the day I was born.

Keep the commas even if you add a day's name.

☑ Friday, April 21, 2015, is a day I'll not soon forget.

You don't need to add a comma when the sentence contains only the month and year.

☑ February 2015 was a disastrous month.

☑ The meeting is set for October 2029, in Philadelphia.

I learned this because in many of my books, I'll list the date and location at the heading of each chapter. I used to use commas to separate month from year until my editor corrected me.

Use a comma when the first word of the sentence is a freestanding "yes" or "no." In other words, you could have stopped with the one-word answer.

☑ I asked my brother if he got chips, and he said, "Yes, I got chips as well as pretzels."

He could have simply said *yes*, but he added more.

Use a comma when directly addressing someone or something in a sentence.

☑ Tommy asked, "Can I go out to play, Mom?"

Use a comma to offset negation in a sentence.

☑ "I made a deposit, not a withdrawal, when I stopped at the bank."

Notice that this is similar to the use of commas with nonessential clauses. If you remove the negative part of the sentence, the meaning of the primary sentence stays the same.

- "I made a deposit when I stopped at the bank."

There are plenty of other rules regarding commas, but most of the common ones are mentioned here. The ones that aren't—like where and when to place commas between adjectives when they are used as descriptors—are easy enough to find.

Part One
WHEN TO USE A COMMA WITH . . .

A while ago, I promised to address the issues many people have when using commas with certain words and phrases. The next few chapters don't cover them all, but they deal with a few of the more confusing ones.

Knowing when and how to use commas is one of the more challenging things to learn about punctuation.

Periods, question marks, exclamation points, and even the others are easy in comparison.

Chapter One
WHEN TO USE A COMMA WITH ...

As Well As

A lot of people pay no attention to commas, and it shows. Commas are critical to reading enjoyment. They instruct readers when to pause or slow down just as other punctuation helps readers know when to get excited or surprised, stop for a long pause, stop-and-go more quickly, etc.

The key to the proper use of commas is knowing when and how to use them. Many writers seem to be confused when to use a comma with "as well as."

Many of the "as" phrases present a problem: "such as," "as in," "as if," "as though," and more. But "as well as" seems to trip people up *as much*, if not more, than the others.

We'll get to those other phrases in time; for now, let's focus on "as well as."

I did a search using Google's Ngram viewer using "as well as" with and without a comma preceding it or following it. The results showed that people used a comma almost as much as they didn't.

Although the results were surprising, they were understandable. "As well as" is used in situations where it doesn't need a comma, but it is also used where it does require one.

The phrase "as well as" is often used to compare things, such as "She's beautiful *as well as* intelligent."

When it's used like this, it doesn't need a comma. But it's also used in ways that do need a comma.

Let's look at a few definitions from *Merriam-Webster's* and Dictionary.com before we go on.

Merriam-Webster's

: and in addition : AND
brave as well as loyal
as well as preposition
Definition of as well as (Entry 2 of 2)
: in addition to : BESIDES
the coach, as well as the team, is ready

Dictionary.com

>as well ,
in addition; also; too:
She insisted on directing the play and on producing it as well. equally: The town grew as well because of its location as because of its superb climate. as well as, as much or as truly as; equally as: Joan is witty as well as intelligent.

Let's look at the examples provided by the dictionaries:

- He's brave *as well as* loyal.
- The coach, *as well as* the team, is ready.
- Joan is witty *as well as* intelligent

In the first example, we're saying he's brave *and* loyal. In that case, no comma is needed. The sentence flows (reads well) without a pause.

In the second example, "as well as the team" seems more like an afterthought. It's like saying "The coach is ready. Oh, yeah, the team is too." You could also read it as "The coach is ready *in addition to* the team."

When you have a similar situation—where the person or item mentioned after "as well as" seems like an *aside* or something *less important*—then you should use a comma.

In the last example: "Joan is pretty as well as intelligent," it seems obvious that "as well as" is used as a conjunction (a connecting word like *and*), and since it is not connecting two independent clauses, no comma is necessary.

Let's look at a few more examples.

- Barbara, *as well as* Tammy, is going to the party.
- Sean and Maddy, *as well as* Nora and Bruce, are going to the beach.
- He doesn't play golf *as well as* his father

In the first and second examples, "as well as" is used to offset two *asides,* so commas are necessary on both sides of the phrase.

Also note how in the first example, even though we mention Barbara and Tammy, we used a singular verb form while in the example with Sean and Maddy, we used a plural.

The reason is because "as well as" does not make the subject a compound subject which would require the plural. This only happens in cases where you combine the nouns, in effect, making more than one subject.

- Barbara and Tammy *are* going to the party.

In the above case, there is no aside simply a conjunction (connecting word) which is used to create multiple subjects: Barbara *and* Tammy.

In the third example, we state "He doesn't play golf *as well as* his father." In that sentence, we're using *as well as* to compare. We're comparing how well he plays golf to how well his father plays. No comma is necessary.

Summary

That sums it up for "as well as" and comma usage.

🐾 If you are adding a phrase or clause and using it as an *aside*, use a comma to offset it. And remember, if that phrase falls in the middle of the sentence, it needs commas on both sides (as we did above). If the phrase comes at the end of the sentence, only use a comma preceding it.

🐾 Any other time you use "as well as," no comma is necessary.

Chapter Two
WHEN TO USE A COMMA WITH BECAUSE

Because is most often used to connect two clauses in a sentence.

- I went to sleep early because I was tired.

You usually don't need a comma before *because*. An exception to this rule applies when the clarity of the sentence is at risk. We'll look at when that may happen later.

Regardless of where *because* falls in the sentence, it is introducing a clause that should answer the question *why*.

- Because it was raining, they didn't go swimming. (*Why* didn't they go swimming?)

That is a dependent clause introducing a complete sentence.

- Because it was raining . . . (dependent clause).
- They didn't go swimming (complete sentence).

In cases where *connecting words*, such as *because, though, since, etc.*, introduce a complete sentence, a comma follows. Now let's look at the reverse.

- They didn't go swimming because it was raining (no comma needed).
- She went to the party because she loved dancing (no comma). (*Why* did she go to the party?)

When a connecting word introduces a dependent clause following a complete sentence, no comma is needed.

And here comes the exception. You knew there'd be one, didn't you?

As I mentioned earlier, exceptions are made if clarity is at risk. When a sentence begins with a negative, it often muddles the clarity of what follows.

- He didn't win the race because of his ego.
- He didn't win the race, because of his ego.

In the first example (no comma), we're implying he won the race but it wasn't due to his ego. (It could have been anything else—someone tripped him, his physical ability, his determination, etc.)

In the second example (with comma), we're implying he *didn't win the race*, and it was *due to* his ego (maybe he hung back too long wanting to show an explosive finish).

- He didn't go for the touchdown because of her.
- He didn't go for the touchdown, because of her.

The same reasoning applies in the above examples.

In the first example, he went for the touchdown, but we're implying the reason he went for it had nothing to do with her. In other words, he went for the touchdown for any number of reasons, but not because of her. He may have had a bet on the game, maybe he wanted to break a record, or perhaps he simply wanted to win.

- He didn't go for the touchdown because of her; he wanted to break the school record.

In the second example, perhaps he didn't go for the touchdown because *she* was rooting for the other team (her school) and he didn't want to embarrass her by padding the score.

You should use commas to clarify as much as possible, but the simpler solution may be to reword the sentence.

- He didn't go for the touchdown because his fiancé was in the stands and rooting for the other team.

Or perhaps there is a more sinister reason why he didn't go for the touchdown.

- He didn't go for the touchdown because he was being paid to shave points.

Just remember, you don't use a comma before *because* with the possible exception of when a negative introduces the sentence. In cases like that, it may be simpler to reword the sentence.

We didn't cover *since*, but it is almost interchangeable with *because*, and in examples like the ones we gave, the same rules apply.

Chapter Three
WHEN TO USE A COMMA WITH SO

One of the more difficult things for me to learn regarding punctuation was when to use a comma with the word *so*.

The use of *so* didn't seem to fit with the normal instances of when to use commas with conjunctions. Sometimes it did and at other times, it didn't. I looked it up in *Garner's Modern American Usage* book and CMOS (*Chicago Manual of Style*).

As is often the case, those explanations left me more confused than when I started.

Finally, I stumbled on an explanation written on Grammarly's site. After reading the blog, I was able to grasp the subtleties of when—and when not to—use a comma with *so*.

I think one of the problems is that *so* is so versatile. It covers a lot of ground for such a little word. Let's look at how it's used.

1. *So* is used as *therefore*, to show the result or consequence of something. (The traffic was bad, so I took another route."
2. *So* is used as *so that*, to show reason or purpose. (He worked hard so she would be proud.)

3. *So* is used to express *addition,* as in "and also." (Times have changed and so has she.)
4. *So* is used as an intensifier, though it's often frowned upon when used that way. (He's *so* cute.)
5. *So* is used to agree or acknowledge the truth of something, as in "I heard it's so."
6. *So* is often used as a substitute for something already stated, as in "She didn't like his manners, and she told him *so.*"

For right now, let's look at the first two usage examples.
The Trick
When you use *so,* substitute *therefore* or "so that" in your head. Say the sentence using those words. If *therefore* works, use a comma; if "so that" works better, do not use a comma. Make sure the sentence retains the same meaning.

One scenario that may mix you up is when you have the words "so that" written in a sentence. I've provided an example below.

- I couldn't care less about Grammarly's suggestion of a dangling modifier, *so that* advice was useless.

The presence of the "so that" phrase may throw you off at first, but if you carefully follow through with the substitution, you'll see it works. Try it with both options, but remember to substitute for *so* only, not for "so that."

- I couldn't care less about Grammarly's suggestion of a dangling modifier *so that that* advice was useless.

- I couldn't care less about Grammarly's suggestion of a dangling modifier, *therefore* that advice was useless.

Therefore is the only substitution that works because you're only substituting for *so,* not for "so that." In other words, if you substituted "so that" the sentence would read as above: "I couldn't care less about Grammarly's suggestion of a dangling modifier, *so that that* advice was useless."

More Examples

- We stayed out all night, *so* we could see the meteor storm pass.

In some instances, the substitution doesn't seem to work. Look at the sentence above. I could substitute "so that" or *therefore* and have either one work.

But if you do the substitutions, and then look closely at the sentences, there is a different meaning depending on which substitution you use.

- We stayed out all night, *therefore* we could see the meteor storm pass.
- We stayed out all night *so that* we could see the meteor storm pass.

In the first sentence, they stayed out all night, and as a *result*, they could see the meteor storm.

In the second sentence, the *reason* they stayed out all night was so they could see the meteor storm.

Two more examples follow.

- We built a fire *so* we kept warm.
- We built a fire, *so* we kept warm.

If you analyze the sentences, you'll see they are similar to those above. In the first sentence, they built a fire *in order* to keep warm (reason or purpose). In the second sentence, they built a fire, and *as a result*, they kept warm.

Substituting *therefore* or "so that" doesn't clarify things enough in the above cases because either one of the substitutions will work.

You have to know what message is being conveyed. Are you trying to tell the *reason* they built the fire? Or are you relating the *result*?

Bottom Line (for this part)

The bottom line is simple. If the sentence works with both substitutions, use a comma with the one that reflects *result* (therefore) and no comma with the one that reflects *reason* (so that).

Other Uses of *So*

When *so* is used as an adverb meaning "to a great extent" or "to a degree," as in "I love you *so* much" or "That felt *so* good" there is no need for a comma before it or immediately following it.

An exception I can think of is if you said something similar to "I love you so, but I can't marry you."

In that case, however, you are adding an independent clause after *so,* and it's that clause that is requiring the comma (preceding *but*).

When *so* is used as a substitute for something already stated, as in "She didn't like his manners, and she told him *so,*" no comma is necessary preceding *so* or following it (assuming words follow it, and no other construction demands a comma). Usually, when used in this manner, *so* comes at the end of a sentence: "Have you finished packing?" "I think *so.*"

When *so* is used to mean "in the same way," no comma is needed, as in "She swam like a fish, and *so* did he."

When used to indicate a measurement (usually accompanied by a gesture), as in "That fish was *so* long" or meaning "to an extent," as in "A man can only do *so* much." In either case, no commas are necessary before or after.

When *so* is used as an introductory word (beginning a sentence), as in "So you finally got here" or "So you arrived!," no commas are needed; in fact, in most cases, *so* isn't needed. Look at the sentences without *so.* "You finally got here" and "You arrived!" Both are fine without *so.*

There are other ways to use *so,* but I can't think of any that would require using a comma immediately preceding or following it.

Chapter Four
WHEN TO USE A COMMA WITH AS

Determining when to use a comma is often difficult, but with the word *as* it seems even more difficult.

Consider the following examples:

- He built a fire *as* it was snowing.
- He built a fire, *as* it was snowing.

Which one is correct? Both.
It depends on the intended meaning. Let's analyze them.

- He built a fire *as* it was snowing.

Without a comma, what we're saying is "He built a fire *while* it was snowing."

- He built a fire, *as* it was snowing.

In this example (with the comma), we're saying "He built a fire *because* it was snowing." The *reason* he built a fire was due to the snow.

Let's look at a few more examples.

- He ate lunch *as* the kids were playing (while).
- He ate lunch, *as* the kids were playing (because).
- Tina yelled for us to come to dinner *as* the baby was crying (while).
- Tina yelled for us to come to dinner, *as* the baby was crying (because).

In the examples above, you can see that when *as* is used in place of *while*, there is no comma, but when it's used in place of *because*, it may need a comma if what follows *as* is nonessential.

Chapter Five

WHEN TO USE A COMMA WITH LIKE AND SUCH AS

This chapter will be slightly different. We'll be discussing *how* to use *like* and "such as" along with how to use commas with them.

Like and "such as" are often used interchangeably and for good reason—they are extremely close in meaning and usage.

I'll repeat this later, but *like* is often used in a comparative mode while "such as" is more inclusive. Let's look at a few examples.

- Dogs such as Great Danes and poodles don't bite.

You don't use a comma before "such as" because it introduces a phrase that is a necessary part of the sentence. We can tell this by removing the phrase to see if the sentence still means the same thing.

- Dogs don't bite.

We all know that's not true. Some dogs *do* bite; therefore, the phrase "such as Great Danes and poodles" is needed.

However, if you said, "Herding dogs, such as Australian shepherds and border collies, are very active," you would need commas. Remove the phrase and see.

- Herding dogs are very active.

Not only does it make sense, it means the same thing. With the phrase intact, we're only adding information, and it's information that isn't needed.

When you use *like* it tells us that what comes before it is to be used in a comparative manner to what comes after it. A few examples follow using both terms.

- She loves long-haired cats, such as the Persian and the ragdoll.
- Her husband loves short-haired dogs, such as the boxer and Dalmatian.
- Her husband loves dogs like the German and Anatolian shepherds, but he can't tolerate the long hair.

Let's look at the sentences above. In the first one, we said, "She loves long-haired cats, such as the Persian and the ragdoll." By using "such as" we indicated that what followed was to be included as examples of *long-haired cats*; in other words, they *were* long-haired cats.

Example two was the same: the Dalmatian and boxer *are* short-haired dogs.

However, in the third example, we said her husband loves dogs *like* the German and Anatolian shepherds, meaning he loves dogs that have something in common with them. Perhaps it is their size, traits, mannerisms, etc., however, he doesn't love the shepherds (they are long-haired dogs) but dogs like them.

Like Is Used for Comparison

We'll go through this again.

While *like* and "such as" are frequently interchangeable, there are differences. *Like* is used to compare what follows, and "such as" includes what follows. Sometimes it may seem like splitting hairs, but if you analyze the sentences, there is a difference. Look at the examples below:

- My grandson loves fruits like strawberries and cantaloupe.
- My grandson loves fruits, such as strawberries, blackberries, cantaloupe, and honeydew.

In the first example, we use *like* to say he loves fruits *that are similar to strawberries and cantaloupe*. It doesn't mean he likes those specific fruits; he may hate *them* but like fruits that are similar.

In the second example, we use "such as" to be specific—saying he loves strawberries, blackberries, cantaloupe, and honeydew.

🖐 Remember to use *like* for comparisons and "such as" when you want to cite examples.

Bottom Line

I don't think anyone is going to misunderstand you if you use *like* instead of "such as" or vice versa, but it helps to know the difference.

Now that I've touted all this nonsense, let me say that *like* and "such as" are as interchangeable as any words I know. I've cited some differences that the strictest grammarians adhere to, but in everyday life, writers can, and should, use whichever word they want.

"Such as" comes across as more formal, and if that's the style a writer is aiming for, they should use it.

If you have a situation where it seems natural to use "such as," then use it. If you think *like* sounds better, use *it*.

Chapter Six

COMMAS WITH "THAT IS," "NAMELY," AND "FOR EXAMPLE"

That is, namely, and *for example* are three expressions that are usually followed by commas, however, there are recommended ways of treating them that differ from the typical practice.

Chicago Manual of Style (CMOS) has the following to say:

> Expressions of the type "that is" are traditionally followed by a comma. They are best preceded by an em dash or a semicolon rather than a comma, or the entire phrase they introduce may be enclosed in parentheses or em dashes.
>
> — CMOS

Let's look at a few examples:

- There are dogs that are far worse biters than pit bulls —*namely*, rat terriers and other small dogs.
- The water district (*that is*, John Moore) voted to increase rates again.
- The water district raised rates again; *that is*, the head of the committee raised them to get his wife a new car.

- Our cat's room held proof of her hunting prowess—*for example*, rat and squirrel tails, remnants of frogs and lizards, and feathers from various birds.

In this same section, CMOS goes on to say:

When *or* is used in a sense analogous to that is (to mean "in other words"), the phrase it introduces is usually set off by commas.

— CMOS

- The surveyor's tool, *or* transit, is used to align points, determine levels, and measure distances.

When *or* is used this way (as "in other words"), it places the phrase it introduces as nonessential, therefore, necessitating commas on either side of the phrase. As you can see in the example, *transit* is merely additional information and not necessary to the sentence.

Chapter One

PERIODS

The period may be the easiest of all punctuation marks to master.

The long and short of it is this: a period ends a sentence. It's similar to a traffic signal that has turned red; it means stop.

If a person has problems dealing with the period, it usually involves the use of a period with other punctuation.

The rules are short and simple. End a sentence with a period. If other punctuation such as a question mark or an exclamation point ends the sentence, then omit the period.

One potentially confusing situation is when a sentence that is not a direct question ends in a quote or when the name of an artistic work requires a question mark. An example would serve best.

- When my kids were younger, they loved the song "Who Let the Dogs Out?"

As you can see, the period was left out even though the sentence was a statement, not a question. The same applies to exclamation points.

Abbreviations are another potential sticking point. Consider the following:

- Don't forget. The meeting starts at 8:30 a.m., so be there.
- Don't forget. The meeting starts at 8:30 a.m.

As you can see, when we remove "so be there" the period following the abbreviation serves as the period that ends the sentence.

Some of the more commonly used abbreviations occur with names. Let's look.

- *Mr.* Johnson will be there; he's giving a speech.
- *Ms.* Simmons will accompany her husband to accept the award.
- And don't forget *Dr. J.* Tomkins starts the evening off at 8:00.

As you can see, periods were required after *Mr., Ms., Dr.*, and the initial *J*.

The proper use of periods with parentheses will be covered in the section dealing with that punctuation mark.

It's just as important to know when *not* to use a period, which isn't often, but it does happen. Many style guides recommend omitting the period after uppercase abbreviations such as FBI, IRS, CBS, HBO, etc; in fact, most initialisms are no longer written that way. A few exceptions are U.S. (United States) or U.S.A. (United States of America). There are others, but those two may be the most recognizable.

If you were to end a sentence with either one of them, the period would be omitted as the example below shows.

☑ I have traveled all over, but I'm glad to be back home in the good old U.S.A.

✗ I have traveled all over, but I'm glad to be back home in the good old U.S.A..

Despite the many rules, the use of periods often boils down to a style choice. Many style guides differ on how words should be punctuated, and I think abbreviations fit that category more than any. Consider some of the variations in geographical terms alone:

- USA or U.S.A.
- UK or U.K.
- Washington DC or Washington D.C.
- NYC or N.Y.C.

No matter the style you choose, it should agree with the style guide you follow. If you don't have a style guide, select a style and be consistent.

Another recommendation for geographical terms is to use periods when referring to American states or Canadian provinces but not when using the two-letter postal abbreviation.

- I went to Col. and Nev. last month, and next month, I'll be going to AZ and UT, if all goes well.

While we're on geography, when writing about the U.S. or the U.K., the full name should be used when they are nouns, but the abbreviations can be used when they're used as adjectives.

- He's from the United States.
- He's a U.S. citizen.
- Her U.K. citizenship is about to be confirmed.
- Her cousins live in the United Kingdom.

Using periods with time indicators or indicators of eras is optional.

- The party starts at 8:00 pm or p.m.
- Julius Caesar died in 44 BC or B.C.
- Augustus Caesar ruled until AD 27 or A.D. 27.

If you have doubt, consult a good dictionary, but be sure to commit to one resource and stick with it, as not all dictionaries agree, and you want to be consistent above all else.

Now on to a topic that remains controversial and often elicits passionate debate.

- Should you use one or two spaces following the end of a sentence?

Thirty or forty years ago, two spaces was the norm; it is no longer the case. A single space is preferred and recommended.

That wraps up periods. The one or two points that weren't covered will be dealt with in those sections.

Chapter Two
QUIZ 1

Punctuation Quiz 1—Commas

The following sentences may or may not have misplaced or omitted punctuation. See if you can spot the issues. And remember, there may be more than one thing wrong in any sentence, or there may be nothing wrong.

1. Sally went home for a nap then decided to stay awake.
2. When Sally went home, she took a nap before dinner.
3. Going home was not her first choice, but once she made the decision she took a nap.
4. Bob went to the store and bought some ice cream and cake.
5. The dog that bit me, the German shepherd, is right over there.

Chapter Three
QUIZ 2

Punctuation Quiz 2—Commas

1. I went to the store and got some milk.
2. When I visited Italy I returned with limoncello.
3. We vacationed in Europe, and bought a lot of clothes.
4. I went to Italy to see the sights, but also the people.
5. I took a train from Rome to Naples and while on the train, I saw Sofia Loren.

Chapter Four

QUESTION MARKS

If the period is the easiest punctuation mark to learn, the question mark may be next in line.

Let's start off with the most common use of a question mark: direct questions.

The rule is as follows.

- Question marks follow direct questions.
- Indirect questions take a period.

Here are a few examples.

- Where are you going? (direct question).
- I wonder where he thinks he's going (indirect question).

For punctuation placement with quotation marks, see that section.

A question mark that completes a book title, song, etc., is retained even if it falls in the middle of the sentence.

- Do your kids like the song "Who Let the Dogs Out?," a one-hit wonder by Baha Men?

- "Who Let the Dogs Out?" is my grandson's favorite song.

If the question mark following the work comes at the end of a sentence, only one end punctuation mark is used.

- My grandson loves "Who Let the Dogs Out?"

If a sentence requiring a question mark is inserted into another sentence, whether it is set off by em dashes, parentheses, or enclosed in quotations, keep the required question mark.

- "He asked me to go to the prom with him. He said, and I quote 'Will you please go with me?,' and of course I said *yes*."
- I wondered where to take her to eat dinner (Should we get Chinese food?), but I decided I should just ask her.
- She told me—Did I hear correctly?—that she'd go to the prom.

Use a question mark when necessary even if it isn't a complete sentence.

- "Her birthday is Monday. Or is it Tuesday? Wednesday? Hell, I don't know."

However, if multiple questions are contained within the same sentence, use only one punctuation mark at the end of the sentence.

- Her birthday is Monday, or is it Tuesday or Wednesday? Hell, I don't know.

Questions That Don't Follow the Rules.
This refers to *requests*. While they may sound like the typical direct question, they are punctuated as if they were an indirect question.

- Will you please put extra cream in that coffee.
- Would someone *please* shut that dog up.

If you're uncertain about a fact when writing, it is often shown by using a question mark within parentheses or brackets to let the reader know of your uncertainty.

- The Pyramid of Cheops was built 4500 (4600?) years ago.

A little bit more on the rule regarding requests. If you ask a favor or make a request that someone *may not* comply with, use a question mark.

When directing a request to someone where the expectation is that they *will* comply, a period should be used (like a wife asking her husband to pick up something at the store). A few examples follow:

- Do you mind telling me your ethnicity and age?
- Would everyone please give a big hand to Susie.

That does it for question marks. If we didn't cover anything here, it will be addressed in the appropriate section.

Chapter Five
EXCLAMATION POINTS

Exclamation points are similar to jalapeños—one or two is fine, but too many are . . . well, too many.

There was an episode of *Seinfeld* where Elaine, who worked at a publishing company, was editing a book, and there was a big argument over the use of exclamation points.

The bottom line is that exclamation points are used for *extreme* emphasis and lose all effect if used too often. The *Oxford English Dictionary* cites the following as one of the reasons to use exclamation points:

> direct speech that represents something shouted or spoken very loudly

Exclamation points by nature denote surprise, anxiety, fright, etc. Because of this, there is no need to state such when using them in dialogue. I often see examples like the following:

- "Call the police!" he yelled (or shouted or screamed).

The use of the exclamation point already tells us he uttered it excitedly. There's no need to tell us again. Some editors may disagree, but from a reader's point of view, I don't want the writer telling me the character yelled or shouted. The exclamation point is enough.

When used, the exclamation point ends the sentence. No other punctuation is necessary.

The use of exclamation points combined with quotation marks is addressed in the discussion on quotation marks.

Chapter Six
QUIZ 3

Punctuation Quiz 3 (Fix the punctuation in each sentence.)
1. I love Italian pastries such as, *cannoli*, *sfogliatelle*, and *pizzelle*.
2. I love Italian food, such as ravioli, lasagna, and gnocchi.
3. I love Italian food, such as ravioli, lasagna, and gnocchi but not dishes that include seafood.

Chapter Seven
QUIZ 4

Punctuation Quiz 4

This one we'll do differently. It will be multiple choice. Choose the sentence or sentences that are punctuated correctly.

The dog was panting, because it had just chased the mailman.
The dog was panting because, it had just chased the mailman.
The dog was panting because it had just chased the mailman.

You'll go to the beach when I say you can young man.
You'll go to the beach, when I say you can, young man.
You'll go to the beach when I say you can, young man.
You'll go to the beach when I say you can young man.

You can't go to the beach and it's because I said so.
You can't go to the beach, and it's because I said so.
You can't go to the beach and it's because, I said so.
You can't go to the beach, and it's because, I said so.

. . .

Cell phones which were a rarity even in the '90s are now everywhere.

Cell phones, which were a rarity even in the '90s are now everywhere.

Cell phones which were a rarity even in the '90s, are now everywhere.

Cell phones, which were a rarity even in the '90s, are now everywhere.

Cell phones, which were a rarity even in the '90's, are now everywhere.

Barbara earned fifty dollars for babysitting but she spent it all on eyeliner and makeup.

Barbara earned fifty dollars for babysitting, but she spent it all on eyeliner, and makeup.

Barbara earned fifty dollars for babysitting but, she spent it all on eyeliner and makeup.

Barbara earned fifty dollars for babysitting but, she spent it all on eyeliner, and makeup.

Barbara earned fifty dollars for babysitting, but she spent it all on eyeliner and makeup.

Chapter Eight
PARENTHESES

Parentheses—When and How to Use Them

I'm guessing most of you know the way to use parentheses, but you may be surprised at some of the rules regarding how to punctuate them. Let's take a look.

The spelling of the word itself is the first thing to look at. *Parentheses* (with an *es* at the end) is plural and is almost always used that way. This differs from *ellipsis* and *ellipses*.

Both words indicate the plural form when spelled with an *es* at the end, but *ellipsis* (singular) *is* the punctuation mark, while *parenthesis* (singular) is only half the punctuation mark.

Parentheses are used to indicate side remarks or to provide additional information. An example follows:

- My black van (the one with the wheelchair ramp) has a handicap license plate.

Remember that whatever is inside the parentheses must not be critical to the sentence; in other words, if you remove what is inside the parentheses, the sentence should still make sense. If you try that with the above sentence, you'll see it works.

- My black van has a handicap license plate.

As you can see, the reader doesn't get the additional information, but the sentence is still complete.

This is the same as what we discussed with *nonessential phrases*, those offset by commas.

Punctuation with Parentheses

Punctuation with parentheses is more complicated. The common practice is to place the punctuation inside the parentheses *if* you've got a complete sentence.

- I wondered where to take her to eat dinner (Should I get Chinese food?), but I decided I should just ask her.

If the parentheses information completes the sentence, place the punctuation outside.

- He went north at the fork in the road (though he could have gone south).

If the words inside the parentheses do not form a complete sentence, then place the punctuation outside the parentheses.

- He came to a fork in the road and paused to think (Which way to go?).

Notice in the sentence above, the period follows the parentheses, while the question mark is inside the parentheses. If a question mark or an exclamation point applies to what is inside the parentheses, they go inside.

Commas almost always follow the parentheses, but not always. If you want to determine whether or not to use a comma, simply take out the parenthetical information and apply the rules we talked about in the section on commas.

- He came to a fork in the road (checked his map), then decided to head north (comma needed).
- He came to a fork in the road, then decided to head north (sentence without parenthetical information).
- He came to a fork in the road (checked his map) and headed north (no comma needed).
- He came to a fork in the road and headed north.

As you can see, punctuation is determined by the structure of the sentence *without* the information within the parentheses.

One thing before we go further. Remember that whatever thought is within the parentheses should not be a primary part of the sentence; in other words, the sentence should stand alone. You should be able to remove the words inside the parentheses and have the sentence still make sense (presuming it made sense before).

Just when you thought you were done, we're going to add a few more rules. If you have a sentence, and you insert a parenthetical thought in the middle which is functioning as an aside or inside comment, you don't capitalize the thought or end it with a period.

- When Sean graduated from college, he was drafted by the Giants (he wanted the Patriots) which upset him.

On the other hand, if the sentence inside the parentheses comes at the end of the original sentence and adds information to the original, it requires an initial capital letter as well as a period at the end, inside the parentheses.

- When the Giants drafted Sean he was upset. (He hoped the Patriots would have chosen him.)

If what you're placing inside the parentheses is an extension of the original sentence or simply explaining something in the sentence, you do not capitalize the initial letter or end it with a period. I'll provide an example from this book.

- Seldom do three letters stir such confusion. And yet it's easy to spot the differences. It's (with apostrophe) is always, and only, a contraction—either for "it is" or "it has," as in "It's been raining" (it has been raining). Or "It's mine" (it is mine).

As you can see "It has been raining" is merely explaining the phrase preceding it: "It's been raining," and the same applies to "It is mine."

Other things to place inside parentheses include:

1. The numbers in numbered lists, such as "Bring these items to the interview: (1) a résumé, (2) a portfolio showing your design work, and (3) a list of references."
2. Area codes for phone numbers: (415) 624-5555. We don't think much about this now as most smartphones and contact-management lists format this automatically.
3. Time zones, which are often cited in emails and other correspondence when arranging interviews. An example follows:

- "The flight leaves at 6:00 p.m. (EST)."

To indicate a person's birth or death date, as in:

- John Lennon (10/9/1940–12/8/1980), was a British (Liverpool) citizen and member of the rock band The Beatles.

To explain the meaning of, or to clarify, an abbreviation or acronym, as in:

- John Smith, the CMO (chief marketing officer) was just promoted again.

PUNCTUATION:

You may also do the reverse. "John Smith, the chief marketing officer (CMO), was just promoted again."

It's only necessary to do this the first time you cite it. The rest of the time, the parentheses are not necessary.

The meaning of the acronym is not capitalized unless it's a proper noun. Note that *chief marketing officer* (above) is lowercase, but if the acronym had represented a proper noun, it would have been capitalized as in the example below.

- When we went to Houston, we visited NASA (National Aeronautics and Space Administration) and saw some interesting videos.

Though seldom used, the following rule is worth mentioning. Translations of a foreign language are often placed in parentheses.

- He claimed to know how to speak Italian, but his vocabulary was limited to *buon giorno* and *buonanotte* (good morning and good night).

A final note on punctuation and capitalization inside parentheses.

If what's inside the parentheses forms a complete sentence, and it ends with a question mark or exclamation point, keep the terminal punctuation (? !), inside the parentheses. Only capitalize the first letter if it's a proper noun or if what is contained inside the parentheses is a quoted sentence, or if it's a complete sentence coming at the end of the main sentence.

- It looked as if we were in trouble. We had good advice (her dad told us "Don't go!"), but we didn't listen.
- It seemed as if he was going to prison for what he did. (Why shouldn't he?)

If the parenthetical sentence ends in a period and occurs mid sentence, *do not* capitalize the first letter (unless it's a proper noun), but still place the period inside the parentheses. If the sentence follows the main sentence, capitalize the initial letter.

One more thing to note. As we already said, the text inside the parentheses is not essential to the sentence and that affects which verb you would use. Look at the following.

- Dana and Nick *are* going to the party.
- Dana (and Nick) *is* going to the party.

In the first example, we're saying both Dana and Nick are going to the party, and there is equal emphasis on each. In that case, a plural verb is necessary because there are two subjects—two people going to the party.

In the second example, the focus is on Dana. *She's* the one going to the party, and oh yeah, Nick is too. In this case, we're saying Dana is going and then adding that Nick is also.

Chapter Nine
ELLIPSES

To start things right, let's get this out of the way—it is *ellipsis* (singular) and *ellipses* (plural).

Ellipses are used to indicate words that have been omitted and, in most fiction writing, pauses in dialogue or narrator thought.

- He wanted to tell her what he'd done, but . . .
- I want to tell you what I've done . . . but I'm afraid you might get angry (pause in thought).
- She was going to be married, but then . . .

Some style guides suggest no spaces either before or after the ellipsis, while others suggest a space preceding and following an ellipsis. Either style works as long as you keep it consistent.

Most writing programs today have a feature that automatically converts three successive periods into an ellipsis, and some editors will accept that. Even with the automatic conversion though, many editors want to see a space between each dot. (Writing programs do the same with two consecutive hyphens—convert them into an em dash.)

An exception many writers make regarding spacing is that if the ellipsis occurs at the end of a sentence, they omit the space after the ellipsis. In the first example below, there is a space before the ellipsis but none after it. The second has a space before and after the ellipsis.

- Jane said, "He wanted to tell her what he'd done, but . . ."
- Jane said, "He wanted to tell her what he'd done, but . . . "

I have to admit, I like it better with no space following the ellipsis.

Note that the *Chicago Manual of Style* (CMOS) suggests spaces on either side of an ellipsis, but AP suggests no spaces. Once again, pick a style guide and be consistent.

Let's look at more of what the style guides have to say. This is from AP:

> In general, treat an ellipsis as a three-letter word, constructed with three periods and two spaces, as shown here.

— ASSOCIATED PRESS STYLEBOOK

AP's recommended formatting is:

- . . .

And not the way writing apps format three periods:

- ...

AP goes on to say:

>Use an ellipsis to indicate the deletion of one or more words in condensing quotes, texts and documents. Be especially careful to avoid deletions that would distort the meaning:

PUNCTUATION:

— ASSOCIATED PRESS STYLEBOOK

- I do solemnly swear that I will faithfully execute . . .

>PUNCTUATION GUIDELINES: If the words that precede an ellipsis constitute a grammatically complete sentence, either in the original or in the condensation, place a period at the end of the last word before the ellipsis. Follow it with a regular space and an ellipsis: I no longer have a strong enough political base. . . . [*sic*]

— ASSOCIATED PRESS STYLEBOOK

The last part of AP's guideline is where a lot of writers go wrong; they use the ellipses only and do not place a period preceding it. If you look above at the example of the presidential oath, you'll see the ellipsis has no period preceding it, but that's because what precedes it is not a complete sentence. If it had been, you would have needed a period followed by a space and an ellipsis.

- I know she loved me. . . .

If what's written is a complete sentence that requires punctuation other than a period, use that punctuation first, followed by a space and ellipsis.

- What if he decides to come? . . .

If an ellipsis is used for deleted words (parts of a speech or quote), and it falls at the end of a paragraph, but is continued at the beginning of the next paragraph, start that paragraph with an ellipsis.

Below is an example taken from *AP Stylebook*'s online site. It cites parts of President Nixon's resignation speech.

>Good evening. ... [*sic*]

In all the decisions I have made in my public life, I have always tried to do what was best for the nation. ... [*sic*]

... However, it has become evident to me that I no longer have a strong enough political base in ... [*sic*] Congress.

— AP STYLEBOOK

The use of the ellipses lets the reader know that parts of the speech have been removed.

By the way, in a couple of the above examples using AP's wording, I used [*sic*] after the ellipsis. I did that because AP had explicitly stated to "treat an ellipsis as a three-letter word, constructed with three periods and two spaces . . ." and yet they continually formatted them as ...

Another Note About Ellipses

If an ellipsis follows a complete sentence, the writer may choose to begin the next letter with a capital even if it didn't start with a capital in the original quote.

- The company announced it was going to begin a new insurance policy on Monday, but it would only be for full-time employees, and, according to Rose, assistant to the CEO, the plan would go into effect immediately.

- The company announced it was going to begin a new insurance policy on Monday. . . . According to Rose, assistant to the CEO, the plan would go into effect immediately.

If you notice, we placed a period after *Monday* (preceding the ellipsis), and we capitalized *According* even though it hadn't been capitalized in the original.

Chapter Ten
QUOTATION MARKS

It wouldn't seem as if quotation marks would be difficult to master, but getting them right takes a bit of learning. Some aspects of usage are easy—like knowing you enclose dialogue within a pair of quotation marks. The following is an example:

- "You can't go to the beach," she said.

That was easy. You put the words someone (she) said inside of the quotation marks.

The more difficult part comes when you add other punctuation. (By the way, I'm using *quote* and *quotation* interchangeably although some people may think that's wrong.)

What kind of punctuation?

Things like periods, commas, question marks, exclamation points, semicolons, colons, em dashes, etc.

Commas and Periods

We'll tackle the easiest ones first: commas and periods. Commas and periods go *inside* the quotation marks, as seen in the previous example.

- "You can't go to the beach," she said.

You could also turn the sentence around and use a period inside the quotation marks.

- She said, "You can't go to the beach."

So the first rule is:

🐗 Periods and commas go *inside* the closing quotation marks (in American English). There are, of course, exceptions, and we'll deal with those later.

By the way, you'll see the wild boar icon (🐗) often. I use it to call attention to rules and such.

Please note that everything discussed here applies to what's known as "American English"; in other words, the English used in the United States, not in countries where British English is used.

There is one exception to this rule. (Isn't there always?) You put commas and periods within quotation marks except when a parenthetical reference follows. To further explain, I'll give you an example from Purdue University's excellent online site.

- According to Foulkes's study, dreams may express "profound aspects of personality" (184).

And here's another one.

Professor Karber's book on "economic crisis" almost caused an "economic crisis" (Karber, p. 255).

Notice that in both sentences the ending punctuation comes after the parentheses and outside the quotation marks.

Another rare exception occurs when you may be providing instructions on how to type something (like a password), and you use quotation marks to designate that. As an example:

- To access the account, type "#,!^@$".

The period has to go outside of the marks so there is no confusion. If the period were inside the quotation marks, it could be considered part of the password.

The above examples are just the type of things I mean when I say you can't say *always*. Many books and sites dedicated to grammar say, "Periods *always* go inside of quotation marks." While I agree that they *usually* go inside, they don't *always* go inside.

Question Marks, Exclamation Points, and Em Dashes

Question marks and exclamation points are the two main forms of punctuation you need to be concerned about, but you can throw em dashes in with them.

These bits of punctuation are the ones with the most flexibility. The accepted rule is that you put a question mark or exclamation point within the quotation marks *if* the punctuation applies to the quotation itself. Place the punctuation *outside* the closing quotation marks if the punctuation applies to the whole sentence. I realize that may be confusing, so I'll provide a few examples:

- His teacher asked him, "Did you do your homework?" (inside)
- Did his teacher actually say, "He did his homework"? (outside)

In the first instance, we're explaining that the teacher asked the student a question. In the second, we are asking if the teacher said what was in quotes. The first sentence is a statement containing a question listed within quotation marks, while the second is a question regarding a statement the teacher made.

Now to tackle em dashes. Em dashes are easier because there is only one easy-to-spot instance when an em dash is used *inside* a quotation mark, and that's when the em dash is used to mark an interruption in dialogue. The following is an example.

- "You better get out of here, or I'll—"
- "Or you'll what?"

That's it. There is no other time I can think of when an em dash would be *inside* the quotation marks (unless it is contained within the sentence).

And now for an example using an em dash outside the quotation marks. Em dashes are seldom used in this manner, but if they need to be, this is how.

- "You shouldn't have betrayed me"—the mob guy slammed his fist on the hood of the car—"but now you'll pay for that."

In the above case, the dialogue is interrupted by *action*. That's why an em dash is required. It could have also been a *thought* as in the following.

- "You shouldn't have betrayed me"—the mob guy thought of what to do next—"but now you'll pay for that."

Or you could have eliminated the em dashes by using a dialogue tag like "the mob guy said."

- "You shouldn't have betrayed me," the mob guy said as he slammed his fist on the hood of the car, "but now you'll pay for that."

This differs from the first example we used because in that sentence, the dialogue was interrupted by another person, so the quotation had to be closed, then reopened with a new speaker. You can see it repeated below.

- "You better get out of here, or I'll—"
- "Or you'll what?"

In the cases where we used the em dash, the dialogue was interrupted by the original speaker. In one case, he interrupted it with action; in the other, it was with thought, but both times the original speaker continued with the dialogue.

Colons and Semicolons

Note that in one of the earlier sentences, when I was explaining the rules governing commas and periods, I used a semicolon that was placed *outside* the quotation marks. I've made note of it again:

- Please note that everything discussed here will apply to what's known as "American English"; in other words, . . .

Another example:

- As Lucky Luciano said, "The mob never dies"; it does get new bosses.

In these examples, the semicolon is placed *outside* the quotation marks because that's where semicolons go. The same applies to colons. Here's an example using a colon:

- The gangster cited three things he attributed to what he called his "rise to fame": tough luck, bad timing, and knowing the right people.

Note:
While researching this, I came across several sites that included "em dashes" with semicolons and colons as punctuation marks that *always* go outside the quotation marks. But as we've seen, that isn't the case. Em dashes have a long history of being used *inside* quotation marks when it comes to interrupting dialogue.

Using Quotation Marks When Referring to Individual Letters

Some writers use quotation marks (as opposed to italics) to emphasize letters when the letters refer to themselves.

- One of the differences between U.S. and U.K. spelling is

how we spell *traveling*. The preferred way to spell it in the United States is with one *l* while in the United Kingdom, it is with two *l*'s.

Note that the last example uses an apostrophe to make the *l* plural. It is one of the few times an apostrophe is used that way (more on that later).

I don't use quotation marks in that manner. I use italics for letters.

Emphasizing Words

Though you technically can use quotes for the same purpose, I like to use italics to emphasize a word and when referring to the word itself because it's less cumbersome, especially when you're setting the definition of a word in quotes.

- The sergeant ordered the men to *move* it. (emphasis)

Also when referring to the word itself.

- When used as a verb *move* means "to reposition something or someone." (referring to the word as itself)

If you notice, in the first sentence the use of italics emphasizes *move* so that as you read the sentence you almost hear the word *move* yelled.

In the second sentence, the use of italics indicates you are referring to the actual word. A good way to test this is to see if you can use "the word" just before the word in quotes:

- When used as a verb (the word) *move* means to reposition something or someone.

Now try it with the first sentence; it doesn't work.

- The sergeant ordered the men to (the word) *move* it.

I never knew this trick until my editor told me. At the time, she was tasked with editing my *No Mistakes Grammar Bites* books, and I had used quotation marks for a lot of words, the ones I wanted to emphasize as well as the ones used as words. Her suggestion made it much easier to read.

Using Scare Quotes

Scare quotes have become popular in the past few decades, and though they sometimes fall out of favor, it hasn't stopped people from using them—possibly even overusing them.

Scare quotes are almost always used to emphasize that a word or short phrase is being used sarcastically or in irony. I've included a few examples.

- She was brutally beaten and almost killed while sleeping at the city's "haven" for battered women.
- He served what he called a "diet" meal, loaded with cheese and cream.

In each case, it is obvious the writer is being sarcastic, and that sarcasm is emphasized by using quotation marks around the word or phrase.

Quotes Within Quotes

This is a tricky one, and although it's seldom used, it's worth noting.

About the only time you'll need this rule is if you're mentioning what someone else said inside a sentence already surrounded by quotation marks; in other words, a "quote within a quote."

If that confuses you, think of it this way: Suppose you're writing a book and a character is talking (which would be inside quotation marks), but what the character says contains a few words someone else said. Below is a character explaining Bill's actions and thought process.

- Sean explained, "Bill was going to tag along, but then

Margaret said, 'It's dangerous,' and her words must have given him pause."

Notice that what Margaret said ('it's dangerous') is surrounded by single quotation marks while the whole sentence (what Joe explained) is surrounded by double quotation marks.

Thin Space

If you are using quotes within quotes, and you wind up with a single quotation followed by a double quotation mark, use a *thin space* to separate them.

If you can't make a thin space (half space) with your keyboard, use a whole space. (I cover how to make a thin space in the chapter titled "Half Spaces.") The following sentence shows when such an instance may occur. It may be difficult to see, but the first example uses a *thin space*, and the second uses a regular space.

- "Dominic's exact words were 'I'm gonna kill him.' "
- "Dominic's exact words were 'I'm gonna kill him.' "

One last thing about quotations: a quote within a quote is repeating what someone else said (but it's written out), and when done in that manner, the word *that* is implied. Here's an example:

- ✗ Jim told us, "Before she died, Mary said *that* 'Their love would last forever.' "
- ✓ Jim told us, "Before she died, Mary said, 'Their love would last forever.' "

Several other times (that I can think of) when single quotes are used are as follows. The first is when a quote is used in a headline. The following is an example:

- The Presidential Candidate Promised 'No More Taxes.'
- Author Says 'Chapter One' of His New Book Will Shock You.

In a normal sentence, "No more taxes" would be enclosed in double quotes (in the United States), but in a headline, it requires single quotes. The same would apply to other things that ordinarily require double quotes, such as song titles or chapters of books, etc.

Please note that in the examples above, the capitalization may not conform to what is required for a headline.

The second is when discussing linguistics or phonetics. If a foreign word is italicized, and if the definition follows, that definition is enclosed in single quotation marks.

- Giorgio is fond of using *ciao*, 'goodbye,' to say hello as well.

Another instance where you should use single quotes . . .

We already discussed that if a quote is inside another quote, you use single quotes to enclose it, but there is another case where you do as well.

Imagine you have a person who has a nickname that you would ordinarily enclose in quotes, such as Nicky "The Rat" Fusco or Tony "The Brain" Sannulo. Now imagine someone mentioning their names while speaking to a third party. An example is below.

- Kate glanced over her shoulder, then looked at Frankie. "Why don't you ask your friend Tony 'The Brain' Sannulo. I'm sure he would know."

The reason for the single quotes instead of double is because it occurs within a sentence wrapped in double quotes already.

Another example would be if a word, meant to be enclosed with double quotes, is used within a quotation:

- Bob said, "When I say 'immediately,' I mean some time before December."

Notice in the example above, the comma goes inside the quotes.

It would be the same if a situation like that occurred at the end of a sentence and required a period.

- Bob said, "I meant sometime before December; that's why I said, 'immediately.'"

And just to clarify, the above is correct with double quotes as well.

✓ The word he said was "immediately."
✗ The word he said was "immediately".

The above example is for those people who use quotes around single words. As I mentioned, I use italics, so for me, that sentence would have read as shown below:

- Bob said, "When I say *immediately*, I mean some time before December."

And yet another time to use them is the following.

For some writing, where the topic is not well-known, the author will use single quotes for words people may not be familiar with:

- The foreman instructed all the bricklayers to 'strike' the joints.

In bricklaying, at least in the Northeast, a commonly referred to practice is "striking," which is nothing more than polishing the mortar joints so they appear smooth.

Another example may be if someone were writing an article or even a book on blackjack (or any specialist topic). They may want to use a blackjack dealer's slang or jargon but are unsure of how many people are familiar with the meaning. Most people know terms such as *bust, double-down, card-counting, push, etc.,* but not many would know what "anchorman" or "first baseman" mean.

An anchorman is the player in the last seat of the table, on the dealer's far right, who is last to act.

A first baseman is the player in the first seat of the table, on the dealer's far left, who is first to act.

Since this is the case, the author may wish to enclose these words in single quotes to distinguish them as words used in that profession.

- In blackjack, the 'first baseman' bets first, and the 'anchorman' goes last.

Quotation Marks Summary

In summary, these are the ways you combine quotation marks with other punctuation marks:

- Semicolons and colons always go *outside* the closing quotation mark.
- Periods and commas usually go *inside* the closing quotation mark (in American English).
- Question marks, exclamation points, and em dashes require you to think about the sentence a little to determine where they go.

And just for grins, here are a few sentences showing the differences between American and British English.

- American: "My love of music began with 'Hey, Jude.' It hooked me."
- British: 'My love of *music* began with "Hey, Jude". It hooked me'.

If you notice, the quotations are reversed, and the period for the British English is placed outside the quotation marks. Here's one more.

- **American**: The word he was looking for was "fulgent."
- **British**: The word he was looking for was 'fulgent'.

For many punctuation issues, the way it's done for British English is the reverse of what is done in the United States; however, you should look it up before finalizing. There may be differences in British English depending on whether it's formal or informal writing.

For the use of single and double quotation marks with measurements, see the chapter on numbers.

Chapter Eleven
QUIZ 5

Quiz 5

   Bill turned to Jean. "That's what she told me. She said, "Do it, or else" and so I did it."
   Bill turned to Jean. "That's what she told me. She said, "Do it, or else." and so I did it."
   Bill turned to Jean. "That's what she told me. She said, 'Do it, or else,' and so I did it."

We should stop and visit Maggie; she lives in Washington D.C.
   We should stop and visit Maggie. She lives in Washington D.C..
   We should stop and visit Maggie; she lives in Washington D.C..
   We should stop and visit Maggie, she lives in Washington D.C.

My kids loved the song, "Who Let the Dogs Out?".
   My kids loved the song "Who Let the Dogs Out?."
   My kids loved the song "Who Let the Dogs Out?"
   My kids loved the song, "Who Let the Dogs Out?."

. . .

Is the traffic bad in D.C.?
> Is the traffic bad in D.C?
> Is the traffic bad in DC?
> Traffic is bad in DC.!
> Traffic is bad in D.C.!
> Traffic is bad in DC!

Chapter Twelve
BRACKETS

First, let's get it straight how to refer to them. Originally, [] were called *brackets* and () were referred to as *parentheses*.

Nowadays, many people are referring to them as *round brackets* () and *square brackets* [], especially in British English. Now back to learning about brackets.

You may go through life and never use brackets, but then again, you *may* find a need for them. In case you do, it would be great to know how to use them.

1. If you're quoting someone else but want to add clarification, use brackets.

Look at the example below.

- I talked to Rose after lunch, and she said, "Tom introduced us to Bob [his brother], but that's as much as I know about him."

You also use brackets to enclose the word *sic* or to make some other comment. In the following example, we're indicating the date was erroneous in the source.

- America was discovered by Columbus in 1592 [*sic*].

When a math problem has more than one level of enclosure to deal with:

- For the physics final, the class was given the following problem to solve. 9[*x* + 5(2 + 4)] = 654.

In the rare event that a third level is needed, you would use {} on the outside, so the order would be: { [( )] }.

Another use for brackets (one of the more frequent uses) is to enclose comments that explain, clarify, or add information to a sentence. It shows that those comments were by the author, and not part of the original quote.

- Steven Spielberg said, "They [the studios] finance for-sure projects only."

In that instance, *they* is clarified by the phrase "the studios," which is contained in the brackets.

Chapter Thirteen
BRACES

I feel safe in saying that unless you're a physicist, mathematician, chemist, or someone of that ilk, you will probably *never* use a brace unless you're playing around.

The only reason to use a brace—that I know of—is to enclose the third level of a nested equation when parentheses and brackets have already been used for the first two, so unless you're working in one of the aforementioned fields, you probably won't run into braces.

There are a few other examples of when braces might be used, although they are not that common:

Examples for Use of Braces:

- Number set: {2, 4, 6, 8, 10, 12} The set of numbers for this problem.
- To list equal choices. Order your favorite ice cream {chocolate, vanilla, or strawberry} and an appropriate cone.

Although I saw some similar things listed as examples, I have never seen braces used this way in real life.

Chapter Fourteen
SEMICOLONS

A Quick Lesson on Semicolons

There are three main circumstances when semicolons should be used.

☀ To join two closely related independent clauses. (This is the primary reason semicolons are used, and it is the way you'll likely see them used most often.)

- John rushed to the store; he had to get milk and bread, or his wife would kill him.

See how the second clause is closely tied to the first? John's life depends on that first clause. The second clause explains why John had to rush to the store.

You could have changed that sentence around a little and still used the semicolon.

- John rushed to the store to get milk and bread; he had to, or his wife would kill him.

☀ To separate lists that include commas.

- John had fifteen minutes to do three things: fill the car with gas; stop and get milk, bread, and a special treat; and get home before the new season of (take your pick) started.

This sentence was full of punctuation: a colon, several semi-colons, a couple of commas, and parentheses. Despite that, I'm hoping it was easy to read. You can thank punctuation for that.

To join two clauses using a conjunctive adverb. (That's why I didn't want to go into detail. Whenever I bring up conjunctive adverbs at parties, everyone walks away.)

I said I wouldn't resort to grammatical terms in these books, so let's forget I said that. The third use of a semicolon is to join two independent thoughts using a word that happens to be an adverb. (I referred to them earlier as connecting words.)

- John had three things to do; however, he decided to take a shower before going.

Some people swear that the dreaded semicolon is a monster and has no place in the modern world. I disagree. I think the semicolon has a few specific purposes, and they benefit us all.

It's okay for writers to play with grammar. You don't have to write in complete sentences. Not all the time. Readers usually know what you mean because people often think that way.

Writers can put periods damn near anywhere. Well. Ma.ybe.

As the preceding example shows, you can't get away with putting periods after every word and certainly not in the middle of a word, but choppy sentences in a novel are fine. Really. They are.

You can even mess up with commas and em dashes or misplace the punctuation inside of parentheses. Readers will assume you are taking liberties as a writer, and they won't worry about it.

Where you run into trouble is when you start messing with

punctuation that most people don't know about, or they only know enough to be dangerous. What am I talking about?

Well, the dreaded semicolon for instance.

The semicolon is so feared that even some editors are afraid of it. I recently had a writer tell me her editors steered her clear of the use of semicolons, going so far as to suggest that one per book was too many.

And Kurt Vonnegut was no friend of the semicolon. This is what Vonnegut had to say:

> Do not use semicolons. They are transvestite hermaphrodites representing absolutely nothing. All they do is show you've been to college.

I'm not sure about the transvestite hermaphrodites, but I'm pretty sure that was not a glowing endorsement.

So why all this talk about semicolons?

I'm here to defend them. I've taken out my sword and drawn a line in the sand; I've had enough. Semicolons are magnificent little creatures that get no respect. Semicolons are like snakes; people fear them, so they kill them.

I'm of a different mindset. I believe semicolons add a special flavor to a well-constructed sentence, a subtlety that a period cannot accomplish.

A well-placed semicolon is precious—like a stolen kiss between secret lovers.

When You Should Use a ;

The following is a repeat a few of the rules we've talked about, but unless you feel you have a solid grasp on the proper use of semicolons, I suggest you read on.

PUNCTUATION: 93

bay bridge

☀ The most common use for a semicolon is to connect two closely related sentences. Think of semicolons like bridges. Imagine Manhattan if there were no bridges connecting it to New Jersey, or Brooklyn, or Queens, or the Bronx. That would make New York an entirely different place. Or suppose San Francisco had no bridge across the bay to Oakland. It wouldn't be thought of as San Francisco/Oakland anymore. It would just be San Francisco. And Oakland.

That's just one of the jobs a semicolon does; it connects two closely related clauses/sentences and brings them closer. Here are some examples:

- I can't eat past midnight tonight; I have to fast for a blood test tomorrow.
- I'm not working in the garden today; I saw a copperhead there this morning.
- Bob drove ninety miles per hour on his way to the hospital; his daughter's life depended on it.

In each of the above, there is a close relationship between the clauses, a relationship that couldn't be served by a comma and wouldn't be served by a period.

Another common use for semicolons is to clarify and separate a list.

- In my book *Murder Takes Time*, there are four main characters: Nicky Fusco, the hit man; Frankie Donovan, the cop; Angela Catrino, the love interest; and Tony Sannullo, the mob guy.

Let's look at that sentence if we used only commas.

- In my book *Murder Takes Time*, there are four main characters: Nicky Fusco, the hit man, Frankie Donovan, the cop, Angela Catrino, the love interest, and Tony Sannullo, the mob guy.

The second example, using all commas, is confusing. Using semicolons clarifies the meaning.

The third instance where you use a semicolon is to join sentences with a conjunctive adverb. Depending on the device you're reading with, either below or on the next page you'll find a list of conjunctive adverbs. This is not a comprehensive list, but it covers many of the more common ones.

accordingly	additionally	also	anyway
besides	certainly	comparitively	consequently
conversely	elsewhere	equally	finally
further	furthermore	hence	henceforth
however	in addition	in comparison	in contrast
incidentally	indeed	instead	Likewise
meanwhile	moreover	namely	nevertheless
next	nonetheless	now	otherwise
rather	similarly	still	subsequently
then	thereafter	therefore	thus
undoubtedly	yet		

For a more robust list of conjunctive adverbs, consult your dictionary or style guide.

- He always wanted to dance; however, he had no coordination.

What You Don't Do with Semicolons

A semicolon should *not* be used in place of a colon. It's not a good substitute, and despite its name association, it doesn't want to be a colon. Semicolons are perfectly content doing the job they were meant to do.

A semicolon should *not* join two unrelated clauses.

Fear of Semicolons

I don't know why people are afraid. Look at them: ;;;;;;; They're not frightening; in fact, they're kind of cute. And it's easy to recognize not only what a semicolon is but what its function is. It is made up of a comma and a period.

The period is on top, so your first inclination is to stop—as if it were a period—but then you see the comma and continue. It couldn't be simpler. If you want to cast blame at the confusion surrounding semicolons, throw stones at the people who named it a semicolon; it would have been better with a name like *periomma*, or *commeriod*.

Chapter Fifteen
COLONS

Use a colon to introduce a list only when following a complete sentence.

An exception may be made when a word or phrase introduces a series or a list, and the verb is *understood*. In such cases a colon is usually required.

Suppose you're making a list of the *pros* and *cons* of something. Instead of writing, "The *pros* are" and "The *cons* are," you could write:

Pros:

- Easy to do
- Inexpensive
- Fast

Cons:

- Won't be able to bill many hours
- Not as good quality
- Hazardous

Now may be the best time to talk about lists since they are often introduced by a colon. Lists are usually unordered (preceded by a bullet) or ordered (number list).

CMOS suggests as its preferred way that if a bulleted list consists of incomplete sentences, that each item can begin with a lowercase letter and does not require a period to end the punctuation (except proper nouns). It further states that if a line carries to the next line, it should be indented. (The following may or may not be indented depending on the device you're reading on.)

- Won't be able to bill many hours which will reduce invoicing.
- Shouldn't have to negotiate hourly rate each time.

In the two examples above, each item was capitalized and each ended with a period. Also each line that carried over was indented.

It's not necessary to keep items lowercase or to eliminate punctuation. Either way works as long as it's consistent.

※ Not all lists should be introduced with a colon. The general rule is that if the introductory text can stand as a grammatically complete sentence, use a colon; otherwise do not. Below are a few examples:

✓ When Jenny comes to spend the night, please have her bring the necessary items: a blanket, a pillow, snacks, any music she wants to listen to, and something to read.

✗ Please send Jenny with: a blanket, a pillow, snacks, any music she wants to listen to, and something to read.

Sometimes it seems as if it's a complete sentence because you're reading the entire thing. To check yourself, read only the part before the colon. In the second example, that would look like this:

- Please send Jenny with:

As you can see, that isn't a complete sentence. Now compare that with the first example.

- When Jenny comes to spend the night, please have her bring the necessary items:

This rule doesn't apply to all situations, but it does to many. A colon should introduce a clause equal to the clause that introduced it. For example, in the sentence above the, "necessary items" Jenny has to bring are the items listed after the colon: a blanket, a pillow, snacks, any music she wants to listen to, and something to read. Let's look at another example.

- They have three black dogs: a poodle, an Australian shepherd, and a mutt.

Notice that what comes after the colon is simply a different way of describing what came before it. It could have been switched. Try it.

- They have a poodle, an Australian shepherd, and a mutt: all three of them black dogs.

When used in this sense, colons function similar to *i.e.,* which is explained in the chapter on Latin expressions.

Colons are also used to separate times, as in 8:30 or 11:00.

There are capitalization rules regarding colons as well. If the clause that follows the colon is not a complete sentence, do not use a capital letter to start it. Here are a couple of examples.

- Here's what I expect: Bring the items I asked for and nothing else.
- Here's what you should bring: gum, coke, and chips.

It's fine to capitalize *bring* in the first sentence (according to

AP), although *Chicago* style is to lowercase after a colon unless what follows consists of *two* or more complete sentences, so *Chicago* wouldn't have capitalized *bring*. If you decide to capitalize any complete sentence, make sure you capitalize all of them. Be consistent.

You do not use a colon when the items listed could be considered part of the sentence. Let's revisit the sentence we used previously:

☑ When Jenny comes to spend the night, please have her bring a blanket, a pillow, snacks, any music she wants to listen to, and something to read.

✗ When Jenny comes to spend the night, please have her bring: a blanket, a pillow, snacks, any music she wants to listen to, and something to read.

The second example had no need for a colon after *bring*. The first example did not contain one.

You may also use a colon between two independent clauses when the second clause explains the first.

- He doesn't have time to learn Italian: he's leaving in less than a month.

The colon is often used for emphasis, and often in lieu of an em dash. While em dashes are preferred by many writers, colons are an acceptable option.

- His trip to Italy could be summed up in one word: magnificent.

The colon is used for other purposes as well.

- To signify the ratio of items—2:5
- To designate passages of the Bible—Leviticus 19:28
- After a salutation—Dear John:

Colons are suggested when formally addressing someone in correspondence, whether that is a salutation or something as simple as a memo.

- Dear Rick: I was going . . .
- Note: Randy, make sure to . . .

Using Colons to Introduce Quotes

There are occasions when you may wish to use colons to introduce quotations: if the material following a colon is very long, you may use a colon to introduce it; if you are reporting on a transcript involving more than one person; if you are citing an interview; it can be used to introduce ongoing dialogue; it can be used when asking a question within the sentence. Examples follow:

Court Transcript

- Judge: "Answer the question."
- Defendant: "I was never at the scene. If someone says I was, they're lying."
- Prosecutor: "If you weren't, then tell us where you were."

Interview

- Detective Johnson: "Tell me how you found the body."
- Ms. Marson: "I came home from the grocery store and found him lying in the kitchen."

A Question Within a Sentence

- As he prepared to take his first skydive he worried: What if the chute doesn't open?

Introducing a Direct Quotation

- Have you read his latest book? I loved the part where the

killer said: "You'll do it now or you won't do anything again."

As a final note, do not use a colon after "such as," "including," and "for example." The use of those phrases are discussed elsewhere.

Part Two
APOSTROPHES

For some people they are the easiest of punctuation items. For others, they seem to be one of the more difficult.

Let's take a look at how they're used and see if we can determine why.

Chapter Two
APOSTROPHES

Maybe it's because apostrophes are so small, but people seem to either ignore or overuse them. Perhaps they think no one will notice.

There are several rules governing apostrophes. Let's take a look.

1. An apostrophe is used to indicate possession.

- Around the corner is Bob's house.
- That used to be Bridgette's car.

There are variations depending on the noun used to indicate possession. If a noun ends in the letter *s* some style guides suggest making it an apostrophe + *s*, while others suggest using an *s,* and then an apostrophe. The sentences below show this.

- Texas' state capital is Austin.
- Texas's state capital is Austin.
- That is the Jones's house.
- That is the Jones' house.

The main thing is to pick a style and be consistent. It should be a style that agrees with the guide you use for other grammatical rules.

Apostrophes are also used in contractions.

- Learning the difference between *it's* and *its* is easy.
- I should've gone with them.

Occasionally apostrophes are used to form plurals but only in a few circumstances.

- Plurals of *lowercase* letters (and four uppercase ones: A, I, M, U) as in: Dot your *i*'s and cross your *t*'s. (See "Italics or Quotation Marks" for details on pluralizing A, I, M, U.)
- Plurals of certain words used as words, as in: "We need to confirm the vote. How many *yes's* and how many *no's* did we have?" (an alternative is *yeses* and *noes*).
- Plurals of certain abbreviations, as in: "The university staff includes sixteen PhD's." (The abbreviation for MD also qualifies for this.)

Please note that depending on the style guide you follow, PhD and MD may or may not use periods in the abbreviation. Some guides recommend Ph.D. and M.D. while others suggest PhD and MD. Either one is fine as long as you remain consistent.

Another common mistake is to use an apostrophe to make a plural where a decade is concerned:

✗ He grew up in the 1960's.
✓ He grew up in the 1960s.

Some people will use 1960's or '50s and it's accepted though not preferred. The main thing, as always, is to be consistent.

Don't make the mistake of using the apostrophe incorrectly when dealing with a noun that is already plural.

✓ The children's party was at noon.

✗ The childrens' party was at noon.

Children is already plural. It means more than one child, so the apostrophe goes after the *n*. We don't add an *s* first.

When using an apostrophe with a phrase like *brother-in-law* think of what you're describing. If you are telling someone about your *brother-in-law's* house, then the apostrophe goes after the phrase, as your brother-in-law is the person who owns the house. If it was a business owned by two brothers-in-law, then the correct way to say it would be my *brothers-in-law's* business.

If two people jointly own the same thing, use an apostrophe for the second person only.

✓ You see that Lexus? It's John and Judy's.

✗ You see that Lexus? It's John's and Judy's.

Do not use an apostrophe with personal pronouns like *hers, its, yours, theirs, whose, ours, mine,* or *his*.

A typographical point more than anything, but be careful not to use a single quotation mark in place of an apostrophe, especially when it comes before a word. I say this because many writing programs automatically correct it in the wrong way. So if you want to start a sentence with the word *because,* but the person is speaking a dialect, you may want to use 'cause. The problem is that even if you hit the right keys, the computer may correct it to 'cause.

More on Apostrophes
Using Apostrophes with Words Ending in S.

While researching the proper use of apostrophes, I came across a practice that was new—at least to me. I was looking for good explanations of when and how to use the apostrophe for words that ended in the letter *s*, and I found what I wanted on grammarbook.com.

Some people use an apostrophe + *s* for every word, and some use an apostrophe for words ending in *s*, but they don't add an extra *s*. And others differentiate depending on whether it is a proper noun. Here are a few examples of how I've seen it done.

- The shark's fin could be seen above the water. (singular)
- The rattlesnake's den was deep in the hillside. (singular)
- The rattlesnakes' den was deep in the hillside. (plural)
- Texas' policy is to prosecute to the full extent of the law. (singular)
- Tobias's beard, and all his hair, had turned white with age. (singular)

Style guides weren't much help; they disagreed with each other as much as they agreed. When I read this article on grammarbook.com, I liked it, and I thought it made sense. You can't ask for more when you're dealing with grammar. They graciously allowed me to copy the following from their site:

> Another widely used technique, the one we favor, is to write the word as we would speak it. For example, since most people saying "Mr. Hastings' pen" would not pronounce an added *s*, we would write *Mr. Hastings' pen* with no added *s*. But most people would pronounce an added *s* in *Jones's*, so we'd write it as we say it: "*Mr. Jones's golf clubs.*" This method explains the punctuation of for goodness' sake.
>
> To show plural possession of a word ending in an *s* or *s* sound, form the plural first; then immediately use the apostrophe.
>   Examples:
>   *the classes' hours*
>   *the Joneses' car (This is different because it is the family car, not just Mr. Jones's car.)*
>   *guys' night out*
>   *two actresses' roles*

Thanks again to grammarbook.com for allowing me to use this.

Even More on Apostrophes
The little apostrophe shouldn't present so many problems, but

it does. Most people understand the concept when it is used with contractions, but some people become confused when presented with issues such as "should I use an apostrophe to pluralize things." (The answer is *no* except in rare situations.) There are also a few cases where an unusual or complex form of possession needs to be expressed. We'll look at a few of these now.

Joint Possession

When people need to refer to joint ownership, there is often a question of where to put the apostrophe. Let's take a look at a few examples as that usually helps.

- ☑ Rose and Jim's horse.
- ☑ Rose's and Jim's horses.

I marked these as both correct because, depending on what you're trying to say, they may both be correct.

In the first example, you're talking about a horse jointly owned by Rose and Jim. There is one horse and Rose and Jim share ownership.

In the second example, by adding an apostrophe to both names, you're talking about multiple horses owned by Rose and Jim separately. (Notice that horses is used in the second sentence, not horse.)

- When you mention one thing owned by more than one person, use an apostrophe with the final (closest) name.
- When you speak about separate things owned by more than one person, use an apostrophe with all the names.
- To make it clear, when two or more people own a single item, place the apostrophe on the last item only.

Before we finish, let's look at a few more examples.

- I love Liz and Chad's kitchen (one kitchen).

- Sahrina and Steve's pool is heated (one pool).
- Nick and Dana's kids are all polite. (The kids belong to them together.)
- Bruce's and Mary's dogs are rambunctious. (Each one has separate dogs.)

However, if either of the parties mentioned is written as a pronoun, use the possessive form for both. Be careful though *not* to use possessive pronouns (mine, yours, hers, his, its, ours, theirs); instead, use possessive adjectives (my, your, her, his, its, our, their). Note that *his* and *its* are common to both groups, so you may have to use them if the situation demands.

I know this rule demands a few examples.

✗ Rose and my horse.

✗ Mine and Rose's horse.

✓ Rose's and my horse.

✓ We went for a ride on his and Rose's horse (*his* meaning Jim).

✗ He and Rose's horse was smaller than most. (*He* is not a possessive.)

✓ Yours and Rose's horse ran quickly.

✗ Rose's and your horse galloped a lot.

If you have a sentence structure that doesn't sound right to you, try rewording it to make it smoother.

Prepositions of Possession

There are three primary prepositions of possession: *of, with, to*. The typical way to use them is shown below.

- *To* is used with a pronoun, such as *it, him,* or *her* (often used with "belongs to").
- *With* is used with an adjective or a noun.
- *Of* is used with a noun or a possessive pronoun, such as *mine, yours, his,* or *hers*.

Here are a few examples:

- The colosseum is a prime example *of* ancient Roman architecture.
- A friend *of my* daughter went on a trip to Greece.
- The boar *with* the sharp tusks has long tusks as well.
- The *Mona Lisa belongs to* Italy, but it resides in France.
- The tomato and basil plants *belong to* my grandfather.

With prepositions of possession, you don't need an apostrophe.

One More Issue

All this talk about apostrophes brings up an example that is often debated. Look at the following sentences. Which is right?

✗ A friend *of* my brother's is coming to dinner.
✓ A friend *of* my brother is coming to dinner.
✓ My brother's friend is coming to dinner.

It should be easy to figure out that the third example is correct, and it is. It's simple; it's your brother's friend. But the other two examples present an issue for some people.

Based on what we just learned, we can see that the second example is the one we're looking for. It uses *of*, one of the prepositions of possession, so *brother* doesn't need an apostrophe.

Now for another example:

✓ The horse *belongs to* Rose and Jim.
✓ The cat *with* Bob is his.

Neither of these needs an apostrophe for the same reason as above.

Before abandoning *apostrophes*, let's look at one more issue. I've seen references to a person's "Achilles' tendon," but there's no need for the apostrophe in that expression. An "Achilles tendon" is a recognized part of the human anatomy, as evidenced by the screenshot taken from W*EbMD's* site.

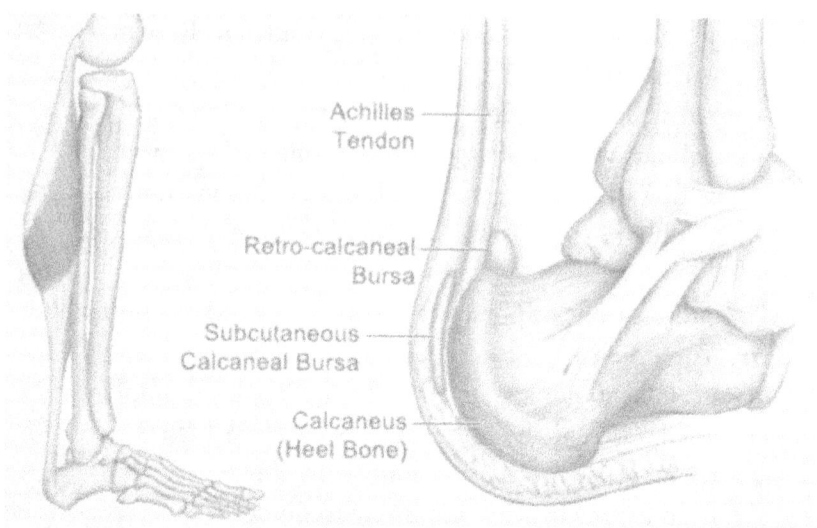

On the other hand, "Achilles' heel" would require an apostrophe because it refers to something symbolic—a seemingly invincible person's weakness (usually a simplistic one). *Merriam-Webster's* has it as an entry and lists it as shown below:

Achilles' heel noun
   Definition of *Achilles' heel*
   : a vulnerable point

— MERRIAM-WEBSTER'S

Many of the British sources I checked with, however, have abandoned the use of the apostrophe with this word. Consider the entry in the *Cambridge English Dictionary*.

a small problem or weakness in a person or system that can result in failure:
   Math has always been my Achilles heel.

The Guardian (British newspaper) has even dropped the capitalization of *Achilles*, and lists it as "achilles heel," without the apostrophe or the capital *A*.

Chapter Three
APOSTROPHES WITH POSSESSIVES

If you have read much, you may have noticed the many times apostrophe use is inconsistent. A couple of words often seen differently are "farmer's market" and "farmers' market" and even "farmers market" with no apostrophe.

I've included a screenshot that shows the results of a search using Google for "farmer's market."

Notice how "Heart of the City . . ." has it listed as "Farmers Market" and in another spot we see "San Francisco Farmers' Market."

Even worse is the treatment received by (arguably) the city's most famous landmark: Fisherman's Wharf. See the screenshots below.

Welcome to San Francisco's Fisherman's Wharf

Notice how in the two screenshots above, "Fisherman's Wharf" is spelled with an apostrophe. In the top one, they have San Francisco in the possessive form also.

But in the two screenshots that follow, you'll see "Fishermans Wharf."

Fishermans Wharf

4.5 ★★★★★ (4,484) · Tourist attraction
286-298 Jefferson St
Buzzing oceanfront tourist center

Hyatt Centric Fishermans Wharf San Francisco

4.3 ★★★★★ (1,794) · Hotel
555 North Point St
Upscale, modern rooms, plus a pool

You have likely seen other phrases, such as "teachers college," "teachers lounge," "homeowners association," "plumbers union," and such.

In all those cases, the words are not being used in a possessive sense but as descriptors, telling what kind of college/lounge, what kind of association, and what kind of union. It's not a college *owned* by teachers but a college *for* teachers.

Different style guides treat this differently. AP says the following:

> Do not add an apostrophe to a word ending in *s* when it is used primarily in a descriptive sense: citizens band radio, a Cincinnati Reds infielder, a teachers college, a teamsters request, a writers guide.

AP also recommends: farmers market, plumbers strike, etc.

Chicago doesn't agree and specifically recommends an apostrophe after *farmers*: "farmers' market."

This disagreement is one more reason why it's wise to pick a guide and stick with it.

Now we'll look at a few more examples based on AP's recommendations.

Descriptive Phrases

Do not add an apostrophe to phrases when they are in use primarily as a descriptor. It's easier to show examples.

- I think CMOS is the best *writers* style guide.
- The New York *Yankees* outfielders are all big men.
- The coal *miners* demand regarding increased wages went ignored.
- His sister is six *months* pregnant.

In the sentences above, the words are not used as possessives as much as descriptors of what follows. It's not the *writers'* style guide, as in a style guide owned by a group of writers; it's describing the kind of style guide—a writers guide as opposed to an editors guide.

The same logic applies to the Yankees. We're not speaking of outfielders owned by the Yankees, we're using *Yankees* to describe the outfielders, to distinguish them from the outfielders who play for the Red Sox or Astros or Dodgers.

And the same goes for the coal miners. We're not speaking of a demand owned by the coal miners; we're describing who made the demand.

It can sometimes be difficult to determine whether to use an apostrophe. One way to test is to see if you can substitute the words *by, for,* or *of.* (You probably have to rearrange the wording.) If *by* or *for* works better, do not use an apostrophe, but if *of* works better, use one. Look at the examples below, which use the sentences we already used.

- I think CMOS is the best *writers* style guide.
- The New York *Yankees* outfielders are all big men.
- The coal *miners* demand regarding increased wages went ignored.
- His sister is six *months* pregnant.

Now let's do some substitution.

- I think CMOS is the best style guide *for* writers.
- The outfielders *for* the New York Yankees are all big men.
- The demand *by* coal miners regarding increased wages went ignored.
- His sister has been pregnant *for* six months.

As you can see, *for* and *by* were easily substituted when the sentences were reworded.

You could have substituted *of* instead of *for* in the sentences dealing with the Yankees and the coal miners, but I don't think the substitution sounds as good.

Let's look at one more:

- The detective didn't believe the witnesses' eyesight, so he continued to question each of them.

I used an apostrophe on this one because it seemed to be more of a possessive statement. Even though the *witnesses eyesight* could be descriptive, it also sounded as if it was possessive. When you do the substitution, it bears that out.

- The detective didn't believe the eyesight *of* the witnesses, so he continued to question each of them.

As you can see, *of* works fine, but *for* and *by* don't work at all.

Plurals Not Ending in *s*

If a plural word does not end in *s* and is in the possessive form, an apostrophe *s* (*'s*) is required.

- Texas *Children's* Hospital
- Young *Men's* Christian Association

Possessive Phrases

In addition, some phrases may be difficult to determine also. One suggestion is to apply the same test we performed above with *of, for,* and *by*.

- A day's wages.
- Three weeks' vacation.
- Two months' severance package.
- Four hours' wait.

Those sayings could be reworded like this:

- A day *of* wages.
- Three weeks *of* vacation.
- Two months *of* severance pay.
- Four hours *of* waiting.

As you can see, *of* worked fine as a substitute in each example, whereas *for* or *by* would have been more difficult to make work (if at all).

Sometimes when a sentence contains both the possessive form of a noun or pronoun as well as a phrase using *of* to indicate possession, it can be confusing.

Look at the example below:

- We went to dinner last night with my sister and a friend of my *brother's*.

The apostrophe is needed after *brother*. Turn it around and see.

- We went to dinner last night with my sister and my *brother's* friend.

Some people may think—Why bother? Just say "a friend of my brother" and be done with it. But that wouldn't be grammatically correct. Because we're talking about *brother* in the possessive form, it needs to be possessive; in other words, it needs an apostrophe.

It may be easier to show if you substitute a pronoun for *brother*.

- *You would say "He is a friend of mine* (mine = possessive)," not *"He is a friend of me."*

Chapter Four
INANIMATE OBJECTS

While we're speaking of *of*, let's look at a few more scenarios where you may use *of* in place of an apostrophe. (That's a lot of *ofs*, isn't it?)

- We were driving across Arizona when the car's engine overheated.

Some people claim inanimate objects shouldn't have a possessive form, as in the case above. But writing the "car's engine" is similar to writing the "engine of the car" except it sounds better. You're not claiming the engine is owned by the car, simply that the engine is part of the car.

Another example would be to say your sick grandmother is at "death's door" or "I'll meet you at heaven's gate." There's nothing wrong with any of those constructions; they're used all the time. I wouldn't go wild using such phrases, but the occasional usage sounds fine.

Chapter Sixteen
QUIZ 6

Quiz 6 (only two of the following are correct)

The onset of the clinical trial showed patients' tolerance for the new drug as "unacceptable;" the conclusion was quite different.

The onset of the clinical trial showed patients' tolerance for the new drug as "unacceptable"; the conclusion was quite different.

The onset of the clinical trial showed patient's tolerance for the new drug as "unacceptable;" the conclusion was quite different.

The third chart from the left, (see figure two), is the correct one.

The third chart from the left (see figure two,) is the correct one.

The third chart from the left (see figure two) is the correct one.

The third chart from the left (See figure two), is the correct one.

The third chart from the left (see figure two), is the correct one.

Part Three
HYPHENS

Most editors will tell you (and they're speaking from experience) that the most frequent errors in spelling occur with compound words. Many people become confused and don't know whether they should use two words, a hyphen between them, or a single word.

Questions regarding hyphenation abound when it comes to spelling, and whether to use a hyphen or one or two words.

The confusion about whether to use one word or two is understandable as the dictionaries often disagree about which version to use. Add to that the fact that many writers spell the words wrong, and it becomes easy to see how confusion sets in.

Chapter Five
TWO WORDS OR ONE?

The screenshot below shows the results of a Google Ngram search for the use of *barcode*, *bar-code*, and *bar code*.

Barcode

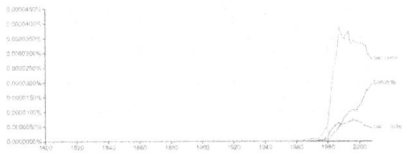

barcode, bar-code, bar code

As you can see from the image, the two-word version is the more commonly used version, although usage is slipping in favor of the one-word version. The hyphenated version is used far less often.

Barcode, Bar Code, or Bar-code?

When you're writing, you might ask yourself—is it *barcode, bar code,* or *bar-code?*

The *OED* (*Oxford English Dictionary*) lists *barcode* as one word. Dictionary.com and Collins Dictionary also list it as one word.

Merriam-Webster's lists it as *bar code,* spelled as two words (as did most of the dictionaries I checked with).

I think most people are familiar with the word *barcode,* so my vote goes for the one-word variation. I don't think there would be any confusion, and when you're writing, and that should be your primary concern.

If you use *Merriam-Webster's*, what do you do? They recommend two words.

In cases like that—even when I feel strongly about the way a word should be used—I still go with my dictionary of choice. It may be begrudgingly, but I do it. It's not often that this happens but sometimes it *does* happen.

If you don't agree, you have plenty of reputable backup: the *OED* lists it as one word, as do *Collins Dictionary*, Dictionary.com, and others.

Hyphenation Questions and Dictionary Recommendations

Dictionaries have a huge effect on how a word is spelled and used, so it's always been a wonder to me why there doesn't seem to be more collaboration. If you look at the Google Ngram results for barcode when using British English, the difference is noticeable. The one-word version is used as often as the two-word variation.

PUNCTUATION:

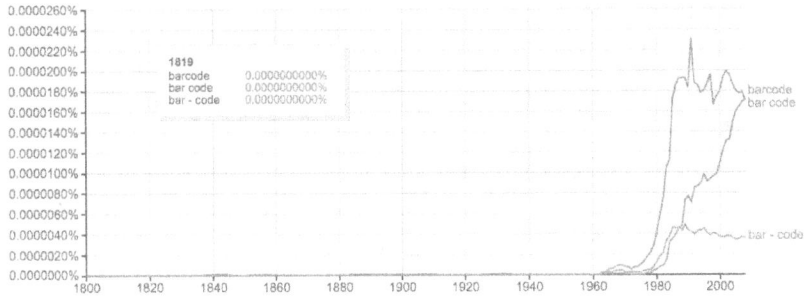

Barcode is one of the easy words, though. You decide on which variation you want to use (one word or two) and stick with it. With some words it's not so easy.

Using Hyphens with Prefixes and Suffixes

Post is always hyphenated when the second part of the word is capitalized, but it appears as one word when that is not the case.

Examples follow:

- post-Victorian
- post-Freudian

But you would say . . .

- postmodern
- postwar
- postdoctorate
- postseason

Words with *wide* at the end (suffixes) are hyphenated when used with proper nouns; otherwise they're not:

- European-wide mandate

But

- statewide

- countrywide
- nationwide

Co Words

Many style guides differ on this rule. I follow AP's suggestion, and that is to retain the hyphen when forming nouns, adjectives, and verbs that indicate occupation or status:

- co-author
- co-chairman
- co-defendant
- co-host
- co-owner
- co-partner
- co-pilot
- co-respondent (in a divorce suit)
- co-signer
- co-sponsor
- co-star
- co-worker

However, AP goes on to say that "several are exceptions to Webster's New World College Dictionary (their dictionary of choice), but in the interests of consistency we used hyphens."

Use no hyphen in other combinations:

- coed
- cooperate
- coeducation
- cooperative
- coequal
- coordinate
- coexist
- coordination
- coexistence

- copay

Cooperate, coordinate and related words are exceptions to the rule that a hyphen is used if a prefix ends in a vowel and the word that follows begins with the same vowel.

Semi Words
No hyphen is used after *semi* unless it is connected to a word beginning with the letter *i*:
- semiconductor
- semicircle

But
- semi-intelligent
- semi-inspirational

Non Prefixes
When faced with words beginning with the prefix *non*, the answer is usually use one word. This wasn't always the case, but there is a trend toward doing away with hyphens, and *non* prefixes are on the list.

While AP recommends almost all words beginning with *non* be one word, they stick with the rule regarding hyphens and proper nouns, so it would be *nonexistent, nonentity*, but he has *non-American* views.

I ran into an issue when writing a book about people who have been successful despite lacking an education—*Uneducated*. It dealt with the use of the word *non-degreed,* which I used frequently throughout the book. None of the dictionaries I checked with had it listed either as hyphenated or one word, and the spellcheckers insisted that the one-word version was wrong.

I finally found it listed as *non degree* in a couple of dictionaries and as one word, *nondegree* in *Merriam-Webster's*.

I couldn't find an answer in CMOS, but in the "Ask the Editor" section of the *AP Stylebook*, it used examples of "non-degreed" and said that if there is the possibility of confusion, use the hyphen.

Up or Down

Compound nouns that end with *up* can be either one word or hyphenated.

Examples follow:

- checkup
- roundup
- pileup
- close-up
- sign-up
- follow-up

This rule applies to nouns, not verbs. So, "I will *follow up* with you next week," but "I'll give you a *follow-up* call."

Most compound nouns that end with *down* are one word. Examples follow:

- breakdown
- countdown
- meltdown
- showdown
- sundown

In and Out.

Compound nouns ending in *in* usually take a hyphen, but compound nouns ending in *out* are usually one word:

- break-in
- buyout
- drive-in
- dropout
- sellout
- sit-in
- standout
- trade-in

Compounds Preceding a Noun

Compounds with *well-*, *ill-*, *better-*, *best-*, *high-*, *little-*, *lesser-*, *low-*, etc., are hyphenated when they precede the noun (unless the expression carries a modifier, such as very).

Examples follow:

✓ Bob is a well-known engineer.
✓ He is well-known in his community.
✓ Susan does high-quality work.
✗ Susan does very high-quality work.
✓ Susan does very high quality work.

Because we used *very* to modify *high-quality*, we remove the hyphen.

In the English language, words are combined in many ways. Even then, the changing isn't done. Often, words continue to change as common usage demands.

A few modern examples of this are: *brunch* (a combination of breakfast and lunch) and *carjack* (a combination of car and hijack, which I hope you have no personal experience with on either side), and *firefly* (a combination of fire and fly).

Often, these words are joined by a hyphen for a while, but invariably they turn into one word. There is only one way to know for certain whether the word is one word, hyphenated, or two words—and that is to look it up in a reliable source. Yet even that isn't as effective as it once was because some dictionaries take longer to recognize a change than others, which is why you will find that one source will cite usage one way while another source will list it as another.

I strongly advise selecting a reputable source and sticking with it. If you're going to use *Merriam-Webster's* as your source, use it every time. If your choice is Dictionary.com, use that every time. No matter what you decide, be consistent.

Do the same with a style book. If you decide to use the *AP Stylebook* as your source, fine. If you decide on the *Chicago Manual of Style* (CMOS), that's okay too.

If you write a lot, you will invariably run into exceptions to the rules. Because of that, I suggest you get a good dictionary and keep it at hand!

Hyphens and Percent

When writing, the word *percent* is always spelled out. You don't write "He showed a 40% increase in sales"; you'd write "He showed a 40 percent increase in sales." There are certain style guides that would advise "forty percent" instead of "40 percent," but the guides agree on spelling out *percent* and not using the symbol.

And there's another thing they agree on—how to hyphenate *percent*. You don't. The word *percent* is always spelled out and never hyphenated. So it's a "20 percent hike" (or "twenty percent"), and not "20-percent" or "twenty-percent."

Hyphenate Words That Use *All*

And do this whether they precede or follow the noun.

Examples follow:

Most religious people will tell you that God is *all-knowing* and *all-seeing*.

She was an all-caring individual. You have to be careful with this because there are some words you might think fall under this rule—like all ready—but they don't, as *all ready* is the preferred choice.

Hyphenate Compound Words Containing Half Whether They Precede or Follow the Noun

Examples follow:

- I looked at Sally during the marketing meeting, and she was only *half-awake*.
- The police made a *half-hearted* attempt to find the burglar.

I cite this rule, but then I'll tell you there are exceptions. If there's anything consistent in grammar, it may be that there are always exceptions. So when you look up words like *half brother* or *half sister*, you'll see they are not hyphenated but listed as two words. So the rule will prevent you from making the combination one word, but it doesn't tell you not to make it two.

Do Not Hyphenate Like Words.

Like words can be listed as one word:

- She maintained her *childlike* sense of enthusiasm, and it made her all the more attractive.

Self Words Should Be Hyphenated:

- self-absorbed
- self-taught
- self-educated
- self-published

There are many more *self-words*, but they are easy to identify, so you should be able to handle it.

Like all grammar rules, there are exceptions, and this one is no different. If *self* is followed by a suffix (selfish, or selfless), or if it's combined with a pronoun (yourself, itself, myself), then those words are not hyphenated.

Words Ending in "ly"

We're going to start with a rule that works *most* of the time, but not always.

Do not hyphenate compound words that come before or after a noun if the word ends in *ly* (and it's an adverb). If it's not an adverb, proceed as normal.

Do not hyphenate compound words containing the word *very* either. So it was a very friendly dog, not a very-friendly dog.

Examples follow:

✗ That's a supposedly-easy exam.
✓ That's a supposedly easy exam.
✗ Her house is an utterly-disgusting mess.
✓ Her house is an utterly disgusting mess.
✗ They went to a family day picnic.
✓ They went to a family-day picnic.

You may wonder why we hyphenated "family-day" when it ends

in *ly*. Because it's not an adverb. The rule states, "Do not hyphenate *ly* words if they're adverbs," but to proceed as normal if they're not. *Family* is not.

Below is a short list of *adjectives* that end in *ly*. They are words that would be hyphenated. I got this list from the GMAT Club site, which helps prepare people for the GMAT (Graduate Management Admission Test).

- bodily
- chilly
- costly
- cowardly
- curly
- deadly
- disorderly
- easterly
- elderly
- family (noun)
- friendly
- ghastly
- ghostly
- grisly
- heavenly
- hilly
- holy
- homely
- jolly
- kindly
- leisurely
- likely
- lively
- lonely
- lovely
- manly
- measly

- melancholy
- miserly
- northerly
- oily
- orderly
- quarterly
- scholarly
- silly
- sly
- smelly
- southerly
- stately
- surly
- timely
- ugly
- unfriendly
- unlikely
- unruly
- unsightly
- untimely
- westerly
- wobbly
- woolly

With any of the words on this list, you *would* use a hyphen, assuming it was a compound modifier.

The same goes for nouns ending in *ly*, and while there aren't as many, I'm sure you will run across them at some time. Here are a few to consider.

- ally
- anomaly
- assembly
- barfly
- belly

- blowfly
- botfly
- bully
- butterfly
- doily
- dolly
- dragonfly
- family
- firefly
- fly
- gadfly
- gully
- hillbilly
- holly
- homily
- horsefly
- jelly
- lily
- mayfly
- medfly
- monopoly
- panoply
- potbelly
- rally
- reply
- supply
- tally
- underbelly

More on Hyphens and When to Use Them

Hyphens seem as if they should be easy to master, but there is a bit of learning to do.

The basics are easy. Hyphens are used to link words together. Classic hyphen usage was to separate things, such as when words at the end of a line reached the margin.

We no longer need to worry about that function. We have computer programs that do it automatically. But there are still hyphenation issues that must be dealt with manually, especially when it comes to compound modifiers.

A compound modifier is made up of two or more words—usually adjectives but sometimes nouns—and those words form a descriptive phrase otherwise known as a compound adjective or compound modifier.

When to Use a Hyphen

There are three main reasons to use hyphens.
- In compound words
- To join prefixes or suffixes to other words
- To show a word break

One more thing—a hyphen is almost always used to join individual letters to words.

- The plumber said we needed a T-joint.
- We drove for miles before coming to the T-junction.
- It was an L-shaped object.
- Once we saw it, we made a U-turn.
- He wore a T-shirt to the wedding!

One rigid rule is that hyphens should not be used as a substitute for en or em dashes. Those dashes have their own purposes and rules, and they should be used accordingly. I've included a look at each one below.
- hyphen -
- en dash –
- em dash —

Another rule is a typographical: hyphens should not have spaces on either side of them, so it's not "re - create," it's "re-create." The same spacing rule holds true with both types of dashes. (CMOS recommends no spaces, *but AP Stylebook* recommends spaces on each side of an em dash.) Once again, I include a sample sentence using each:

- He claimed to be a hands-on manager (hyphen).
- He worked at Apple from 1999–2006 (en dash).
- She's a sympathetic—or empathetic—sort of person (em dash).

Clarification

The other function of the hyphen, and perhaps the most important, is to provide clarification or remove confusion. At it's simplest form, it's to clarify a word that may otherwise be confused with a similar-sounding word. A few classic examples are:

- recover and re-cover
- reform and re-form
- repress and re-press

Without the hyphen, *recover* means "to find or get back," as in "He recovered the stolen jewelry" or "to recover from an illness," as in "He had a heart attack, but he recovered."

With the hyphen, *re-cover* means to place new fabric on a chair or sofa or something similar, as in:

- She re-covered the antique chair with new material.
- Many things can be re-covered even books.

There is a lot of confusion when it comes to compound words. Here is an article I did on compound words, and here is the list available as a download. The main thing to understand is that a hyphen is used to clarify your meaning.

👉 A tip: you typically hyphenate two or more words that come before a noun and present a single idea; however, you do not need to hyphenate them if they come after a noun. The sentences below may help to explain this:

- She was a runner and loved to run a *long distance*.

- She was a runner and loved *long-distance* races (long-distance is describing the kind of race).
- He often called his wife from France, which was a *long distance* away.
- He often made *long-distance* calls to his wife.
- He was a *self-made* man, having been born into the working class.
- He was a *working-class* man.
- You should *back up* your data so that if your computer crashes, you'll have a *backup*.

In the first few sentences, I hope the examples are self-explanatory—the hyphenated version is a compound adjective—it describes what kind of races and what kind of phone calls. In the third sentence, the hyphenated word describes the kind of man, a working-class man.

The fourth sentence is different. It shows the difference between using a one-word version versus a two-word version.

And so you know, *back up*, when used as a verb is always two words, but you'd say:

- "The army unit called for *backup*."
- "He made a *backup* of his hard drive."

As much as some people insist on using a hyphen with *backup* it doesn't make it right. Here is an example :

✗ "Make sure you copy everything to your *back-up* drive."

The hyphen is not needed, and, as you can see by usage results from a Google Ngram search, the use of *backup* as one word far exceeds *back-up*. Some people still use a hyphenated version, and if it's used as a replacement for the one-word version, it's not a huge error, but you should never use it as a replacement for the verb, the two-word version.

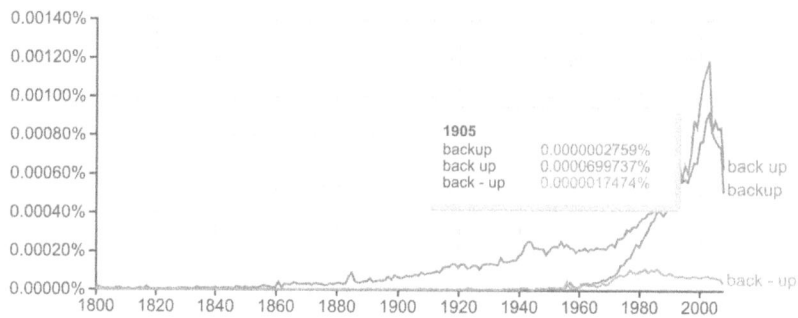

Here are a few of sentences to wrap up our discussion on when to use *back up* versus *backup*:

- He was the *backup* quarterback, and as such, he sat on the sidelines a lot.
- The police officer was under fire, so he called for *backup*.
- You should heed his advice and *back up* your hard drive.

As you can see, when used as an adjective to describe something else, such as "backup quarterback," it's one word. When used as a noun—a person, place, or thing, such as "He called for backup,"—it's one word. But if used as a verb, denoting action, it's two words, as in "Back up your hard drive."

More Clarification

The main goal of writing should be to clarify things; in other words, convey your thoughts in the easiest, clearest manner possible. With that in mind, the proper use of hyphens goes a long way. Consider the following:

- She is an *infectious disease* doctor.
- She is an *infectious-disease* doctor.

In the first sentence, we're claiming she is a disease doctor who is infectious, and in the second sentence, we're claiming she is a doctor who deals with infectious diseases. That's a big difference. I think I'd prefer being treated by the second one.

Other Uses

Remember that hyphens can be used with more than one word. Their purpose is to provide clarity, and whether two, or three, or more words are needed for clarification makes no difference. Below are a few sentences that demonstrate this.

- Coffee is often considered a *pick-me-up* because of the effect caffeine has on some people.
- My *brother-in-law* recently bought a new car.

In both cases, we were speaking of one thing so a hyphen was needed to join the words to make it one thing.

Hyphens to join prefixes and suffixes to words

Whether we're talking about hyphens used to join compound words or about hyphens used for prefixes and suffixes, they're still being used to join words. And one of a hyphen's jobs is to do just that.

We've already talked about hyphens when used with a few *re* words. Now let's look at a few other rules of hyphen use regarding prefixes and suffixes.

Hyphens are also often used in words using *re* or *pre* that result in two of the same kind of vowels next to each other such as *re-engage* or *re-evaluate*. If we didn't hyphenate them, we'd have *reengage* and *reevaluate*, both of which are wrong. I found one dictionary that listed *reevaluate* as an alternative way to spell *re-evaluate*, but none of the dictionaries had *reengage* listed. It was consistently listed as *re-engage*.

Below are a few more words with a *re* prefix that require hyphens:

- re-extend
- re-establish
- re-encounter
- re-enable
- re-emphasise

- re-elevate

The above list consists of words that definitely need a hyphen.

Subjective Hyphen Use

Hyphens are often used subjectively; in other words, it's left up to the writer whether to use a hyphen or not. In more cases than not, the determining factor is clarity: If you think a hyphen will help make you message clearer, use it; if not, don't. Let's look a little deeper at that aspect of hyphenation.

There are a few rigid rules regarding hyphens, but often it's up to you. Many prefixed words can be written with a hyphen or without one. The school of thought is to avoid a hyphen with a prefix; however, if you feel the word looks awkward without a hyphen, or if your spellchecker flags it as wrong, use a hyphen.

A good example is the word *antiaircraft*. All the dictionaries I checked with listed it as one word—no hyphens—and yet many times writers hyphenate it.

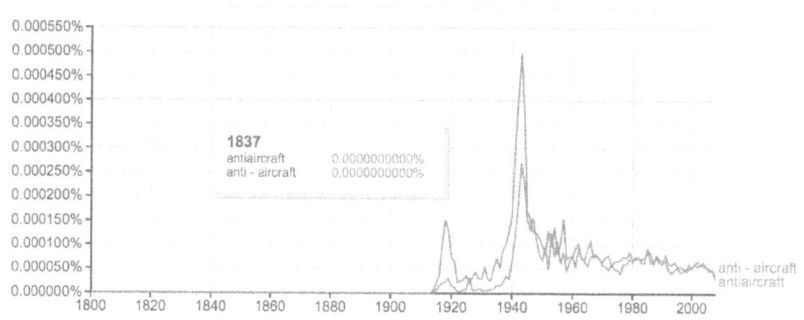

The above screenshot is the result of a Google Ngram search. As you can see, usage in general has dropped off dramatically, but when it was used, the hyphenated version (anti-aircraft) far outweighed the one-word version.

The bottom line is that using *antiaircraft* is not wrong, and you will find authoritative backup if you go that way, but if you're like many people, you may think it looks awkward and choose to hyphenate it. That's what the subjective use of hyphens is all about.

In the next chapter, I've listed a lot of compound words, many that are hyphenated and many that aren't. Below is a list of words beginning with *anti* that AP recommends using without hyphens as they have specific meanings.

antibiotic	antibody	anticlimax
anticoagulant	antidepressant	antidote
antifreeze	antigen	antihistamine
antiknock	Antimatter	antimony
antioxidant	antiparticle	antipasto
antiperspirant	antiphon	antiphony
antipollution	antipsychotic	antiserum
antiseptic	antithesis	antitoxin
antitrust	antitussive	

More Rules

A couple of these rules will be a repeat of what you've already learned.

1. If your prefix sits before a proper noun, use a hyphen: post-Nixon era, pre-Kennedy politics.

2. Do not allow the same vowel to double up: re-enter, re-evaluate. This is a rule with exceptions as evidenced by *preempt*. There are other exceptions, particularly when the vowel is an *o*. If you don't mind how the word looks without a hyphen then omit it. But if you do mind, leave the hyphen in.

The image below displays the Ngram search results for *cooperate/co-operate* and *coordinate/co-ordinate*. You can see that the majority of people use those words without the hyphen, though many do use the hyphen.

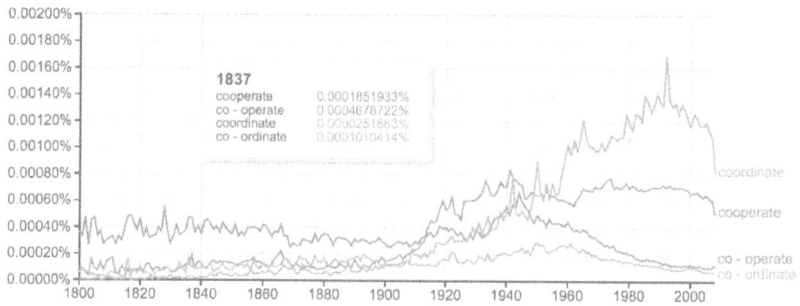

Sometimes your spellchecker may flag a word. Usually, it's best to accept the suggestion, but if you have doubts, check whatever dictionary you use. The final decision is yours. If you feel you need a hyphen to clarify words or to make them look better, use one.

1. Use a hyphen with *ex*

The prefix *ex* is usually followed by a hyphen:

- ex-husband
- ex-lover

Hyphens with *Fold*

If you're using *fold* and spelling out the number before it, use it without a hyphen, such as "a threefold increase"; however, if you're using numerals with *fold*, use a hyphen, as in "a 120-fold increase in the rodent population."

1. Also use hyphens anytime that the base word is:

- Capitalized
- A number
- An abbreviation
- When using two or more words to describe the same thing.

Below are a few sample sentences showing the above rules.

- He was voting in the pre-Nixon era.

- Heroin has been a problem since post-1990s
- He hasn't been around since pre-CIA.
- I want to compete in all the races: the two-, five-, and ten-meter runs.

That about covers it. If you question whether a word should or should not include a hyphen, look it up in your favorite dictionary, although they don't always agree.

Because of that, I'll give the same advice I do for other matters, like style guides. Pick a dictionary you like and stick with it.

Trends

There continues to be a tendency to shy away from hyphenated words, despite the demand for clarification. *Oxford English Dictionaries* reports that approximately sixteen thousand hyphenated words were removed in their latest edition, being replaced in most instances by the one-word variation, but sometimes two words. Oxford rigorously maintains that clarity is paramount. Here's an example.

- When we traveled to San Francisco, we saw *five-hundred-year-old* trees.
- When we traveled to San Francisco, we saw *five hundred year-old* trees.

In the first sentence, you're saying that you saw trees that were five-hundred years old. In the second sentence, you could be saying you saw five hundred trees that were a year old. You could further confuse this by saying:

- When we traveled to San Francisco, we saw five *hundred-year-old* trees.

In this case, you'd be saying you say five trees that were a hundred years old. So you see, the diminutive hyphen, much like the comma, *does* matter.

Hyphens Used with Years

Because we just discussed this, it may be a good time to cover how hyphens are used with years.

If the age is used as an adjective or as a substitute for a noun, then it should be hyphenated.

Example:

- He's a *24-year-old* intern.
- The dog is *three years old*.
- The game is for *six-year-olds*.

The Bottom Line

There are plenty of other rules and reasons why you do or don't use a hyphen. If you follow this guide, you'll be right most of the time, but you're still better off consulting a dictionary. You're always going to run into situations like *good night*, which can be found in three forms:

- *Goodnight*, dear. I'm going to bed.
- He gave her a *good-night* kiss.
- Their team won, so it turned out to be a *good night*.

Or how about these:

- I'm looking for the best *work-out* equipment.
- I just had a great *workout*.
- I'm going to the gym to *work out*.

Each one of the above six sentences is correct. It all depends how the word is used.

Exceptions

We've talked about a few exceptions, and there are more, but I felt it wise to mention at least one more as it is frequently used.

We cited an earlier rule that stated, "Don't use hyphens with adverbs as a part of compound modifiers." One exception is the word "well." The following sentences are all correct.

- He prefers the *well-known* brands of coffee.
- She wasn't a *well-known* person until after the election.

But you don't hyphenate them if they come after the noun, similar to other compound modifiers.

- Her books are *well known* in England.
- The Marlborough brand of cigarettes is *well known* throughout the world.

The difference is when you use *well-known before the noun, it is being used as an adjective.*

One Last Rule

I know I said *one* last rule, but this is a three-part rule, so bear with me.

1. When it comes to compound verbs, that is, when two or more nouns are combined to form a verb, the resulting word is hyphenated. Keep in mind, this applies to nouns that are combined to form verbs; it doesn't apply to all words. So the following is correct:

- Be careful, the place is one big *booby trap* (noun).
- Be sure to *booby-trap* (nouns combined to form verb) the cabin before we leave.

Don't use hyphens when the word is made of a verb and an adverb or a preposition (like *up, in, on,* etc.). A few examples follow.

- If you save ten dollars a day, you will quickly *build up* your savings.

- Your wife called. She said, "Don't forget to *drop off* the prescriptions."

3. If the above-mentioned words are used as a noun and not verbs, use a hyphen.

- The pipe was clogged due to a *build-up* of grease.
- The kidnappers were specific regarding where to make the *drop-off*.

I hope that helps. But please remember that if you're in doubt about anything, consult a dictionary or style guide.

A Little Help

How many times have you typed a word or were about to type a word, when you asked yourself—*Is that two words or one? Or does it need a hyphen?*

I don't know about you, but it happens to me all of the time. And, as we've mentioned, the spellcheckers don't always agree.

The question of whether to use two words or one comes up more times than you may think. And when you add hyphens to the mix, it becomes damn frequent—frequent enough to cost you a lot of time to ensure you get it right.

That's why, in this chapter, I'm going to include a long list of oft-questioned words. Feel free to use this list as a reference. It will be a lot faster than consulting a dictionary.

In fact, to make things even faster, I use a key combination (shortcut) linked to my list, so if I'm typing and have a question, all I have to do is type *hyphenwords*, (with no spaces), and it immediately takes me to the list. You can learn all about how to save precious time by using text shortcuts in the book I wrote about that—*No Mistakes Writing, Volume I—Writing Shortcuts*.

The Oxford-English Dictionary website addresses the issue of compound words and sheds some light on their usage. It shows that many of today's single-word forms, such as those listed below, were originally written as separate words.

- forever
- tomorrow
- instead
- nonetheless
- somewhat
- whatsoever

The merging of words appears to be a strong trend in American English, where it's standard practice to write *underway*, *anymore*, or *someday* as one word, whereas the two-word forms are still the norm in British English.

Compound words are primed for confusion, yet in most cases—at least in conversation—they do *not* cause confusion. Even in writing, they seldom make anyone stop and think, though they may make a person wonder about your grasp of the language.

What do I mean?

If you write, "I had *alot* to eat for dinner," people may know you used the word erroneously, but they will still know that *alot* means for *a lot*.

It's when we delve into other words where the meaning is different between the one-word and two-word version that we run into problems.

One of these is the first word on our list: along. *Along* and *a long* have different meanings. Let's take a look.

Along or a Long?

Let's look at these examples to understand the difference:

✓ The art critic should have seen that mistake *a long* time ago (correct).

As you can see, you cannot substitute *along* for that, or you'll have:

✗ The art critic should have seen that mistake *along* time ago (incorrect).

Similarly, look at these opposite examples.

✓ I held the umbrella for her as she walked *along* with me (correct).

✗ I held the umbrella for her as she walked *a long* with me (incorrect).

The two-word version is meant more as a measurement of time or distance, as in "He lives *a long* way off" or "Christmas is *a long* time away."

Along can mean several things, one of them is "beside or next to," as in "The sidewalk along the meandering creek."

Alot or A lot?

This one is easy, and yet I still see it misused *a lot*. It's easy to get right because *alot* is not a word. The way to write it is always as two words.

Any more or Anymore

Any more (two words) is reserved for "even the smallest amount," as in "I don't want any more to drink."

Anymore (one word) is reserved for "any longer." In other words, when used as an adverb, the one-word spelling *anymore* is used, as in "I don't go there anymore."

Whether there are an equal number of people using *any more* as there are *anymore* in the proper sense, I don't know. But proper or not, their usage is almost equal. It's also obvious that the one-word version has gained massive popularity during the past forty years.

Any Place or Anyplace

As you can see from the chart below, the proper usage of *any place* as two words has been slipping when compared to *anyplace* as one word. *Anyplace* as one word has been accepted for informal speech for a while, but it has been frowned upon in formal writing.

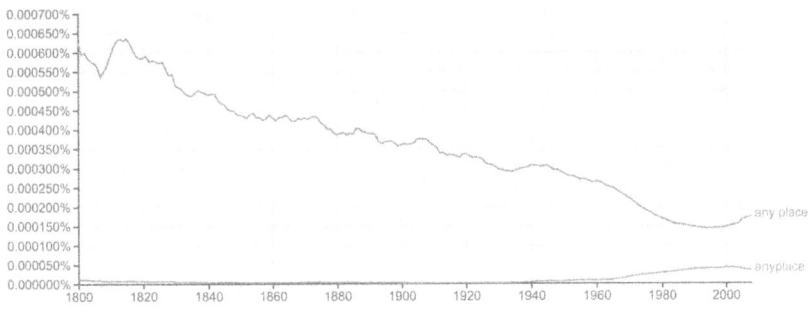

Any Time or Anytime

During the past twenty years, *anytime* has made headway but it is still far behind its two-word counterpart when it comes to usage.

Apart or a Part?

Apart means separated by a distance of time or space, as in "Dallas and Fort Worth are thirty miles *apart*" and "The innocent man stood *apart* from the others."

A *part* is a piece of something, a component, as in "I went to Auto Zone to get *a part* for my car."

🐾 The way to remember this (and some others) is by testing it with the plural use. *Apart* cannot be used in the plural sense. Try it. Dallas and Fort Worth are thirty miles *aparts*. That doesn't make sense.

However, "I went to Auto Zone to get three *parts* for my car" makes perfect sense.

If you can use a plural and still have it make sense, it's the two-word version. This works for other words also (mostly ones that use *a* as an indefinite article. Try it with the next example—*apiece* and *a piece*.

Apiece or A piece?

Apiece is used for an expression meaning "each." It's an adverb and means "for each one," as in "Give them one apple apiece (each)."

A piece refers to a piece of something, as in "I'd love a piece of that pie."

👉 Remember that *a piece* is two words and refers to something that has, or had, more than one piece or part. *Apiece* is one word and refers to just one.

Best Seller or Bestseller or Best-seller

Merriam-Webster's lists it as two words. Dictionary.com lists it as one word, but offers the two-word option as an alternative. And Cambridge lists only the one-word option.

My editor uses the two-word option for a noun, although when it is used as an adjective, she hyphenates it. So it would be *best-selling*, as in "She is a best-selling author" or "That is a best-selling book." But when used as a noun, it would be the two-word option, as in "He is a best seller."

Broken-down or Broken Down

Every source I checked had it hyphenated: *broken-down*.

Copyeditor or Copy Editor?

Dictionary.com lists it either way, but *Merriam-Webster's* lists only the two-word version. The Free Dictionary lists both ways, while the *AP Stylebook* claims it is two words.

If the dictionaries and style books can't agree, how are we to know which is right?

Extensive research will only exhaust you. It seems like most resources recommend *copy editor* as two words, but few disapprove of the one-word variation. I would say—like so many compound words—that either form will work, but I would still go with the two-word option; that's what the American Copy Editor Society suggests.

👉 The way I remember it is to remind myself that a copy editor is an editor that edits copy.

Copyright or Copy Right or Copywrite?

According to the *AP Stylebook*, a *copyright* (one word) is:

> ... the exclusive right to make copies, license, and otherwise exploit a literary, musical, or artistic work, whether printed, audio,

video, etc.: works granted such right by law on or after January 1, 1978, are protected for the lifetime of the author or creator and for a period of 70 years after his or her death.

🔖 The way I remember it is simple. A copyright is one thing, so it's one word.

Copywrite

Copywrite is a rarely used derivative of copywriter—which refers to a writer of copy (used mostly in advertising). Most people would consider this an error, so you're safer saying that someone writes copy rather than that they copywrite.

🔖 The way I remember it is simple. A *copyright* is one thing, so it's one word.

Double Check or Double-Check

Cambridge dictionary lists it as a verb and hyphenated. *Merriam-Webster's* lists it both ways, the noun form (a *double check*) and the verb form (*double-check that*). Dictionary.com lists the verb and noun as hyphenated, but also lists the noun without hyphens.

I think you're safe if you use hyphenated, but to be *doubly safe*, I'd use hyphenated for the verb and two words for the noun form.

So . . .

- Please *double-check* that work.

But . . .

- Before you leave for the day, do a *double check* on the data.

E-book, ebook, eBook

As a term for books presented in electronic form, *eBook* is going out of style, at least in edited publications. As of early 2012, most American, Canadian, and Australian news publications that publish online are using the hyphenated, uncapitalized form: *e-book*. Meanwhile, most web-friendly British publications are using the one-word: *ebook*.

Login or Log in?

Login and *log in* have different meanings depending on whether they are used as a noun, adjective, or verbal phrase:

- —the place where you enter your username and password is the login page (adjective).
- —the information you use may be known as your login (noun).
- —but the action of signing on is called logging in (verb), as in "Log in to your account to access it."

🔊 One way to tell the verb form is if you can place a word between *log* and *in*, as in "The system will *log you in* automatically."

Nevermind or Never Mind?

Now let's tackle the ever-popular *never mind*. Or is it *nevermind?*

It is used so much as one word it's in danger of becoming accepted, but most spellcheckers still flag it when used as one word, and right they are. *Never mind* is meant to be used as two words, meaning "forget about it" or "pay it no mind."

In some instances, it's obviously meant to be used as two words:

- "It's going to be a scorcher today," her husband said. "That's okay. I never mind the heat."

When *never mind* is used like the above, it seems apparent that it is used appropriately. But there are cases where usage comes into question.

Nevermind as one-word has been creeping into the vocabulary, especially when used in the following context:

- "You want me to lock the door when I leave?" he asked.
- "Nevermind," she said. "I'll get it myself."

To set the record straight, *never mind* should be used as two words, but I wouldn't worry about it if you let it slip by as one.

Recent research has shown that *nevermind* as a one-word alternative is used fifty percent as much as the proper way, using two words. When the popular usage gets that high, it typically isn't long before it becomes recognized as an accepted way to express yourself.

🔔 The way I remember it is to think of the alternatives: "pay no attention," "pay no mind," "forget about it," etc., are all more than one word. And *never mind* is more than one word.

On-line or Online

There was a time when *on-line* was okay. Now usage favors *online*, used as one word.

Overtime or Over Time

Over time is used as follows: "I'll get to fixing that fence over time" (meaning "someday" or "over the course of time").

Overtime, as one word, means putting in extra hours. "He had ten hours of overtime last week."

Someday or Some Day?

This one is not a huge mix-up, but some people *do* get it confused, so let's take a look at it.

Someday is used for an indefinite time in the future, as in "*Someday* my ship will come in." Or "*Someday* I'll meet Mr. Right."

This is unspecific, only naming the future as a time when it will happen.

"Some day" is for a *specific* day that hasn't been named. as in "We'll go to the zoo *some day* next week." That statement tells you that it will be next week, but it doesn't name the day. Or, "*Some day* next month we'll visit the college dorms."

Start-up or Startup

This one is hotly debated, and there are many proponents on both sides. If you poll the major newspapers, *startup* seems to win, however, *start-up* isn't far behind. In fact, if you use Google's Ngram to compare, it's almost even, with *start-up* gaining ground in the past few years.

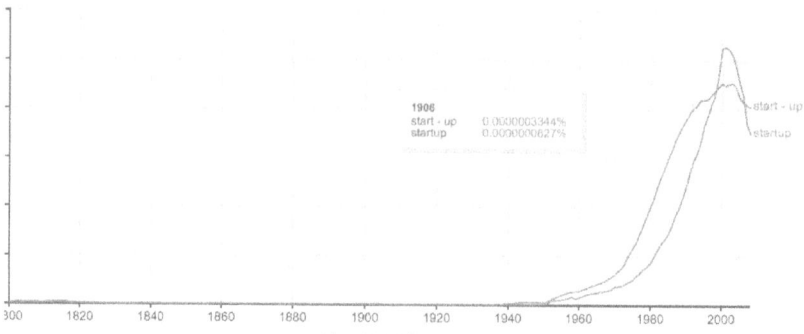

The people I spoke with about this seemed to favor *start-up* when it was used to describe a company, as in "Apple was a successful *start-up* company." But the favor shifted to *startup* for other usage. "Apple was once a garage-based *startup*."

Telltale or Tell-Tale or Tell Tale

This one was less controversial than I thought. Everywhere I checked, all agreed that it should be one word: *telltale*.

That surprised me because I see it so often as a hyphenated word, such as a *tell-tale sign,* but apparently, it should be a *telltale sign*.

All resources I checked with showed *telltale* as one word, yet the most famous example I know of using *telltale* is Edgar Allen Poe's short story "The Tell-Tale Heart," which uses a hyphenated version.

Rule of Thumb for All Words

A good rule to remember is that the verb form of a compound word is usually two words, or sometimes hyphenated. The noun form is usually one word, and the adjective form is usually hyphenated (or one word).

Examples are as follows:

- Noun (and adjective)—"Do the cleanup, and then you can go home."
- Verb—"Clean up that mess before you leave."

The bottom line is that common usage is forcing more words

than ever to evolve from two words or hyphenated words into one, but there are instances when things go the other way.

Examples of hyphenated words that have become two words are below. The first is one we're all familiar with. It's presented in the form of a screenshot from *Merriam-Webster's*.

income tax
noun

screenshot of income tax

Merriam-Webster's listing of "income tax" without hyphens.

I highlighted *income tax*, but there are more than a few words that have gone this route: *ice cream, high school*, and more.

Even when used as an adjectival phrase, the words remain separate. "He was a high school senior," not "He was a high-school senior." And "She was enjoying her ice cream cone," not "She was enjoying her ice-cream cone."

There remain a few holdouts, people who insist on the hyphen, but almost all credible sources agree that the hyphen is no longer needed.

Chapter Six
MORE OF TWO WORDS OR ONE

Here is a list of words that can be either one or two words or possibly hyphenated.

- able-bodied
- about-face
- aboveboard
- absent-minded
- ad-lib (n.,v.,adj.)
- after-hours
- aftereffect
- afterglow
- after-hours
- afterimage
- afterlife
- afternoon
- afterthought
- aide-de-camp
- air base
- air show
- air time

- air-conditioned
- aircraft
- airfield
- airlift
- airline
- airmail
- airmen
- airplane
- airport
- airtight
- airtime
- airways
- a la carte
- a la king
- a la mode
- all ready
- already
- all-knowing
- all-seeing
- all-encompassing
- all-compassionate
- all-forgiving
- all ready
- all right
- all-time (n)
- all-time (adj)
- allover
- allspice
- alma mater
- alongside
- a lot
- already
- also
- also-ran (n)
- another

- anti-aircraft
- anti-bias
- antibiotic
- antibody
- anticlimax
- antidote
- antifreeze
- antigen
- antihistamine
- anti-inflation
- anti-intellectual
- anti-labor
- anti-slavery
- anti-social
- anti-war
- antibiotic
- antibody
- anticlimax
- antidote
- antifreeze
- antigen
- antihistamine
- antiknock
- antimatter
- antimony
- antiparticle
- antipasto
- antiperspirant
- antiproton
- antiseptic
- antiserum
- antithesis
- antitoxin
- antitrust
- antitussive

PUNCTUATION:

- anybody
- anyhow
- anymore
- anyone
- anyplace
- anytime
- anyway
- anywhere
- archbishop
- archdiocese
- archenemy
- archrival
- around
- art form
- art work
- artifact
- ashcan
- ashtray
- attorney general
- auto racing
- automaker
- autoworker
- awe-struck
- awhile (adv)
- baby sitter
- baby-sit
- baby-sitting
- babysitter
- back porch (n)
- back seat (n)
- back street (n)
- back up (v)
- backup (n)
- back yard (n)
- backache

- backbite
- backbone
- backbreaker
- backcountry
- backdrop
- backfire
- background
- backhand
- backhanded
- backlash
- backlog
- backpack
- back porch (n)
- back-porch (adj)
- backseat (adj)
- back seat (n)
- backside
- backslap
- backslide
- backspace
- backspin
- backstabbing
- backstage
- backstop
- back street (n)
- back-street
- backstroke
- backtrack
- backward
- backwoods
- backyard (adj and noun)
- bail out (v)
- bailout (n)
- ball carrier
- ball point pen

- ballclub
- ballpark
- ballplayer
- ballroom
- Band-Aid (trademark)
- bandleader
- bank robber
- bankbook
- bankroll
- bar mitzvah
- barhop
- barkeeper
- barmaid
- barrelhouse
- barroom
- barstool
- baseball
- basket case
- basketball
- beachcomb
- became
- because
- become
- bedclothes
- bedrock
- bedroll
- bedroom
- bellbottom
- bellboy
- bellhop
- bellybutton
- below
- best seller
- best-selling
- big time (n)

- Big-time (adj or adv)
- big-bang theory
- big-time (adj)
- bird watching
- bird's-eye
- blackball
- blackberries
- blackbird
- blackboard
- blackjack
- blacklist
- blackmail
- blackout
- blackout
- blacksmith
- blacktop
- blast off (v)
- blastoff (n adj))
- blood bath
- bloodhound
- blow up (v)
- blow-dryer
- blowgun
- blowup (n)
- blue blood (n)
- blue chip stock
- blue-blooded (adj)
- bluebell
- blueberry
- bluebird
- bluefish
- bluegrass
- blueprint
- boarding school
- boardinghouse

- boardroom
- boardwalk
- bodybuilder
- bodyguard
- bodywork
- boldface
- bona fide
- bonbon
- boo-boo
- bookcase
- bookdealer
- bookend
- bookkeeper
- bookmark
- bookmobile
- bookseller
- bookshelf
- bookstore
- bookworm
- boomtown
- bootstrap
- bowlegged
- bowlegs
- bowtie
- box office (n)
- box-office (adj)
- boyfriend
- brainchild
- brainwash
- brand-new
- break dancing (n)
- break in (v)
- break-out
- break up (v)
- break-dancing

- break-in (n adj))
- breakdown
- breakup (n adj)
- breast-feed
- bricklayer
- bridegroom
- bridesmaid
- broken-down
- brother-in-law
- brothers-in-law
- brownout
- brussels sprouts
- bugspray
- build up (v)
- buildup (n adj)
- bull's-eye
- bullet hole
- bulletproof
- bullfight
- bullpen
- Bundt cake
- bus line
- businesslike
- businessman
- businesswoman
- busload
- butterball
- buttercup
- butterfingers
- butterflies
- buttermilk
- butternut
- butterscotch
- buy out (v n)
- by-election

- bylaw
- byline
- bypass
- byproduct
- bystreet
- cabdriver
- cabinetmaker
- cakewalk
- call up (v)
- cameraman
- cancan
- candleholder
- candlelight
- candlemaker
- candlestick
- cannot
- car pool
- car seat
- card maker
- cardboard
- cardsharp
- cardstock
- carefree
- carefree
- caretaker
- careworn
- carfare
- cargo
- carhop
- carload
- carmaker
- carpetbagger
- carpool
- carport
- carrack

- carry over (v)
- carry-over (n)
- carryall
- carsick
- carsick
- cartwheel
- carwash
- caseload
- cash flow
- cashbox
- cast member
- catch all (v)
- catchall (n adj)
- cattail
- catwalk
- caveman
- cease fire (v)
- cease-fire (n)
- centerfold
- cha-cha
- chain saw
- chairman
- chairwoman
- change over (v)
- change up (v)
- change-up
- changeover (n)
- check up (v)
- checkup
- check in (v)
- check-in (n)
- check out (v)
- checkout (n)
- cheese maker
- cheeseburger

- cheesecake
- chief
- chock-full
- chowhound
- Christmastime
- church member
- churchgoer
- citizens band
- city hall
- citywide
- claptrap
- clean up (v)
- clean-cut
- cleanup (noun)
- clear-cut
- clearinghouse
- cloak-and-dagger
- clockwise
- close-up (n adj)
- closed shop
- co-author
- co-chairman
- co-host
- co-owner
- co-partner
- co-pilot
- co-respondent
- co-signer
- co-star
- co-worker
- coal mine
- coastline
- coatdress
- coattails
- Coca-Cola

- coed
- coeducation
- coexist
- coexistence
- coffee grinder
- coffee maker
- coffee table (n)
- coffeemaker
- coffeepot
- coleslaw
- colorblind
- comeback
- comedown
- commander in
- commonplace
- commonwealth
- con man
- concertgoer
- Confinement
- congressman
- congresswoman
- cooperate
- coordinate
- coordination
- cop-out
- copy desk
- copy editor
- cornmeal
- cornstarch
- cost-effective
- countdown
- counter top (n)
- counter-top
- counteract
- countercharge

PUNCTUATION: 171

- counterfoil
- counterproposal
- counterspy
- country-martial
- country-western
- countryside
- courthouse
- courtroom
- courtyard
- cover up (v)
- crack up
- crackup (n adj)
- crawfish
- crawl space
- crew member
- crewcut
- crisscross
- crock pot
- cropland
- cross country (n)
- cross fire
- cross over (v)
- cross section (n)
- cross-country
- cross-examination
- cross-examine
- cross-eye
- cross-section (v)
- crossbow
- crossbreed
- crosscut
- crossover
- crosswalk
- curtain raiser
- custom-made

- cut back (v)
- cut off (v)
- cutoff
- cut out (v)
- cutback (n adj)
- cutoffs
- cutout (n)
- D-day
- dairymaid
- daisywheel
- daisywheel
- dark horse
- date line
- day to day (adv)
- day-to-day (adj)
- daybed
- daybook
- daybreak
- daycare and day-care
- daydream
- daylight
- daylong
- daytime
- dead center
- dead end (n)
- dead-end (adj)
- deadline
- deathbed
- decade-long
- decision maker
- decision-making
- deep water (n)
- deep-sea (adj)
- deep-water
- Deepfreeze (trademark)

- degree-day
- derring-do
- desk top (n)
- desk-top (adj)
- die-hard (n adj)
- dinner table
- disease
- dishcloth
- dishpan
- dishwasher
- dishwater
- disk drive
- ditchdigger
- docudrama
- doghouse
- dogwood
- dollhouse
- door to door (n)
- doorstop
- double bind
- double-check
- double-faced
- double-parked
- down-home
- downbeat
- downdraft
- downside
- down under
- drawbridge
- drive in (v)
- drive-in (n adj)
- driveway
- drop out (v)
- duckbill
- duckpin

- duckweed
- dump truck
- Dutch oven
- Dutch treat
- dyed-in-the-wool
- earache
- eardrop
- eardrum
- earmark (v)
- earring
- earthbound
- earthquake
- earthward
- earthworm
- easygoing
- ebook
- e-book
- e-Book
- editor in chief
- egghead
- eggshell
- elsewhere
- email
- e-mail (I prefer this version but you can use any)
- empty-handed
- en route
- every day (adv)
- every one (each
- everyday (adj)
- everything
- extra-base hit
- extra-dry
- extra-large
- extra-mild
- extralegal

- extramarital
- extraterrestrial
- eye to eye (adv)
- eyeballs
- eyeglasses
- eyelash
- eyelid
- eyesight
- eyesore
- eyewitness
- face lift
- face to face (adv)
- face-to-face
- fact-finding
- fade out (v)
- fade-out (n)
- fall out (v)
- fallout (n)
- far-fetched
- far-flung
- far-off
- far-ranging
- fare up (v)
- farm worker
- farmhouse
- farmland
- farsighted
- father-in-law
- fatherland
- feather bedding
- feather-bedding
- fee-table (adj)
- Ferris wheel
- ferryboat
- fiberglass

- field house
- field trip
- fieldwork
- film ratings
- film-making
- filmgoer
- filmmaker
- filmmaking (n)
- fingertip
- fire breather
- fire chief
- fire wagon
- firearm
- fireball
- fireboat
- firebomb
- firebreak
- firecracker
- firefighter
- fireflies
- firehouse
- fireproof
- firetruck
- firewater
- fireworks
- firsthand
- fishbowl
- fishbowl
- fishbowl
- fisherman
- fisheye
- fishhook
- fishlike
- fishmonger
- fishnet

- fishpond
- fishtail
- fistfight
- flagpole
- flagship
- flameout
- flare-up (v)
- flea market
- flimflam
- flip-flop
- floor-length
- flower girl
- flyswatter
- folk singer
- folk song
- follow up (v)
- follow-through
- follow-up (n
- foolproof
- foot-and-mouth
- football
- foothill
- footlights
- footlocker
- footnote
- footprints
- footrest
- forbearer
- forbid
- fore-topgallant
- fore-topmast
- fore-topsail
- forearm
- forebear
- forebrain

- forecast
- foreclose
- foreclosure
- foredoom
- forefather
- forefeet
- forefinger
- forefoot
- forego
- foregoing
- foregone
- foreground
- forehand
- forehead
- foreknowledge
- foreleg
- foreman
- foremost
- forepaws
- foresee
- foreshadow
- foresight
- forestall
- forethought
- foretold
- forever
- forewarn
- foreword
- forget
- forgive
- forklift
- format
- fortnight
- fortuneteller
- fortunetelling

- forty-nine or '49er
- foul up (v)
- foul-up (n)
- four-flush
- frame up (v)
- frame-up (n)
- free on board
- free-for-all
- free-lance (v adj)
- free-lancer (n)
- freestanding
- freewheeling
- freewill offering
- freeze-dried
- freeze-dry
- freeze-drying
- friendship
- front line (n)
- front page (n)
- front-line (adj)
- front-page (adj)
- front-runner
- fruit grower
- fruit cup
- full house
- full page (n)
- full time (n)
- full-time (adv)
- full-dress
- full-fledged
- full-length
- full-page (adj)
- full-scale
- full-size (adj)
- full-time (adj)

- fund raising (n)
- fund-raiser (n)
- fund-raising (adj)
- G-string
- game plan
- gearshift
- get together (v)
- get-together (n)
- gift wrap (n)
- gift-wrap (v)
- giveaway
- glass (generic)
- glassmaking
- go ahead (v)
- go-ahead (n)
- go-go
- godchild
- goddaughter
- goodbye
- goodnight
- goose bumps
- grandaunt
- grandchild
- grandchildren
- granddad
- granddaughter
- grandfather
- grandmaster
- grandmother
- grandnephew
- grandnieces
- grandparent
- grandson
- grandstand
- granduncle

- grasshopper
- grassland
- graveyard
- ground rules
- ground water
- groundbreaking
- groundskeeper
- groundswell
- grown-up (n adj)
- guesthouse
- gumball
- gun battle
- gunboat
- gunfight
- gunfire
- gunpoint
- gunpowder
- H-bomb
- hair dryer
- haircut
- hairsbreadth
- hairstyle
- hairstyling
- hairstylist
- half dollar
- half note
- half sister
- half size (n)
- half sole (n)
- half tide
- half-baked
- half-blood
- half-brother
- half-cocked
- half-hour (n adj)

- half-life
- half-mast
- half-moon
- half-size (adj)
- half-sole (v)
- half-staff
- half-truth
- halfback
- halfhearted
- halftime
- halftone
- halftrack
- hamburger
- hammerhead
- hand to hand (n)
- hand to mouth (n)
- hand warmers
- hand-carved
- hand-held
- hand-painted
- hand-picked
- hand-set (v)
- hand-sewn
- hand-stitched
- hand-to-hand (adj)
- hand-to-mouth
- handbook
- handcrafted
- handcuff
- handgun
- handhold
- handmade
- handout
- hands off (n)
- hands-off (adj)

- handset (n)
- handwrought
- hang up (v)
- hang-up (n)
- hangover
- hanky-panky
- hard-bound
- hard-cover
- hard-line
- hardback
- hardworking
- harebrained
- harelip
- has been (v)
- has-been (n)
- head-on
- headache
- headdress
- headlight
- headline
- headlong
- headquarters
- heart-rending
- heartbeat
- heartfelt
- heartwarming
- helter-skelter
- hereafter
- hereby
- herein
- hereupon
- herself
- heydey
- hi-fi
- hide out (v)

- hide-out (n)
- hideaway
- high jinks
- high point
- high-rise (n adj)
- high-step (v)
- high-stepper (n)
- highball
- highchair
- higher-up
- highland
- highway
- himself
- hit and run (v)
- hit man
- hit-and-run (n)
- hitchhike
- hitchhiker
- ho-hum
- hoar-long
- hocus-pocus
- hodgepodge
- hold over (v)
- hold up (v)
- holdup (n)
- holdover (n)
- holdup (n adj)
- home builder
- home buyer
- home-baked
- home-grown
- homemade
- homemaker
- homeowner
- hometown

- honeybee
- honeycomb
- honeydew
- honeymoon
- honeysuckle
- hook up (v)
- hookup (n)
- hookworm
- horse race
- horse rider
- horse-trader
- horseback
- horsefly
- horsehair
- horseman
- horseplay
- horsepower
- horseradish
- hot line
- hot seat
- hot spot
- hot tub
- hotbed
- hotheaded
- house call
- houseboat
- housecleaning
- household
- househusband
- housekeeper
- houseplant
- housetop
- housework
- however
- hurly-burly

- hush-hush
- hydroelectric
- hyperactive
- hypercritical
- ice storm
- in-depth
- in-group
- in-house
- in-law
- inasmuch
- inbound
- individual
- Indochina
- indoor (adj)
- indoors (adv)
- infield
- infighting
- infrared
- infrastructure
- inpatient (n adj)
- inside
- insofar
- intake
- inter-American
- international
- interracial
- interstate
- intramural
- intrastate
- ironwork
- itself
- jackpot
- jai alai
- jailbait
- jellybean

PUNCTUATION:

- jellyfish
- jerry-built
- jet plane
- jetliner
- jetport
- job hunting (n)
- job-hunting
- jukebox
- jumbo jet
- jump shot
- jury-rigged
- Kmart
- keyboard
- keyhole
- keynote
- keypad
- keypunch
- keystone
- keystroke
- keyway
- keyword
- kick off (v)
- kickoff (n)
- kilowatt-hour
- kindhearted
- knock off (v)
- knock-off (n)
- know-how
- kowtow
- lad
- lame duck (n)
- lame-duck (adj)
- lamebrain
- last-ditch effort
- latecomer

- lawsuit
- left wing (n)
- left-handed
- left-hander
- left-wing (adj)
- let up (v)
- letup (n adj)
- life jacket
- Life Savers (trademark)
- life vest
- life-size
- lifeblood
- lifeboat
- lifeguard
- lifelike
- lifeline
- lifelong
- lifesaver
- lifestyle
- lifetime
- lifework
- lift off (v)
- liftoff (n)
- light bulb
- light-year
- lighthearted
- like-minded
- like-natured
- likewise
- limelight
- limestone
- long distance (n)
- long shot (n)
- long term (n)
- long time (n)

- long-distance
- long-lasting
- long-lived
- long-range
- long-run
- long-shot (adj)
- long-term (adj)
- longhand
- longhouse
- longstanding
- longtime (adj)
- look-alike
- lovemaking
- lukewarm
- lumberyard
- lunch box
- lunchtime
- machine gun (n)
- machine-gun
- machine-gunner
- machine-made
- mah-jongg
- mainland
- mainline
- make up (v)
- makeshift
- makeup (n ad))
- man-made
- map maker
- meantime
- meanwhile
- meat loaf
- meatball
- meat cutter
- *ménage a trois*

- menswear
- mental
- merry-go-round
- metalwork
- mid-America
- mid-Atlantic
- midterm
- mind-set
- mine shaft
- miners
- minibus
- miniseries
- miniskirt
- mix up (v)
- mix-up (n)
- mock-up (n)
- money-saving
- moneymaker
- monthlong
- moonbeam
- moonlight (n v)
- moonlit
- moonscape
- moonshine
- moonstruck
- moonwalk
- mop up (v)
- mop-up (n adj)
- moreover
- mothball
- mother-in-law
- motherhood
- motor home
- motorcycle
- mountain man

- mousehole
- movie house
- moviegoer
- moviemaker
- moviemaking
- mud slide
- multicolored
- multilateral
- multimillion
- multimillionaire
- muscle ache
- music
- nail clippers
- name tag
- narrow gauge (n)
- narrow-gauge
- narrow-minded
- nationwide
- nearby
- nerve-racking
- nevermore
- new wave (n)
- new-wave (adj)
- newborn
- newfangled
- newfound
- news writer
- news writing
- newsboy
- newsbreak
- newscaster
- news dealer
- newsletter
- newsmagazine
- newsman

- newspaper
- newsperson
- newsprint
- newsreel
- newsroom
- newsstand
- newsworthy
- nickname
- night shift
- nightclub
- nightfall
- nightspot
- nighttime
- nitpicking
- nitty-gritty
- no one
- nobody
- noisemaker
- nonaligned
- nonrestrictive
- nonchalance
- nonchalant
- nondescript
- nonentity
- nonsense
- nonsensical
- northeast
- notebook
- noteworthy
- nowhere
- nursemaid
- nutcracker
- oceangoing
- oddsmaker
- off-Broadway

- off-color
- off-duty
- off-off-Broadway
- off-peak
- off-road
- off-season
- off-white
- offhand
- offset
- offshore
- offside
- offstage
- oilman
- old times
- Old West
- Old World
- old-time
- old-timer
- on-line
- one time (n)
- one-sided
- one-time
- oneself
- onetime
- ongoing
- only
- open-minded
- out of bounds (n)
- out of court (adv)
- out-of-bounds
- out-of-court
- outact
- outargue
- outbluff
- outbox

- outbrag
- outclimb
- outdated
- outdistance
- outdrink
- outfield
- outfight
- outfox
- outhit
- outleap
- outmatch
- outpatient (n adj)
- outperform
- outpitch
- outpost
- outproduce
- output
- outrace
- outscore
- outshout
- outstrip
- outswim
- outtalk
- outwalk
- ovenproof
- overabundance
- overall
- overboard
- overbuy
- overcoat
- overexert
- overflow
- overland
- overrate
- override

- overshoes
- oversize
- overtime
- overview
- pacemaker
- pacesetter
- paddy wagon
- painkiller
- pancake
- panchromatic
- pantheism
- pantsuit
- pantyhose
- Pap test (or smear)
- paper bag
- paper clip
- paper towel
- paperwork
- pari-mutuel
- parkland
- part time (adv)
- part-time
- partygoer
- passbook
- passerby
- passkey
- Passover
- passport
- patrolman
- patrolwoman
- paycheck
- paycheck
- payday
- payload
- peace offering

- peacekeeper
- peacekeeping
- peacemaker
- peacemaking
- peacetime
- pell-mell
- pen pal
- penny-wise
- peppermint
- percent
- pet store
- petty officer
- pickup
- pile up (v)
- pileup (n adj)
- pillowcase
- pin up (v)
- pinch hit
- ping
- Ping-Pong (trademark)
- ping-pong (v) as a verb, no caps
- pinhole
- pinstripe
- pinup
- pinup (n)
- pinwheel
- pipeline
- place mat
- playback
- playboy
- playhouse
- playoff
- playthings
- pocket watch
- pocketbook

- point-blank
- police officer
- policy-maker
- policy-making
- policyholder
- pom-pom
- pompon
- ponytail
- pooh-pooh
- popcorn
- post office
- postcard
- postdate
- postdoctoral
- postgraduate
- postnuptial
- postoperative
- postscript
- postwar
- pothole
- potluck
- potshot
- powder keg
- power line
- pre-convention
- pre-cut
- pre-dawn
- pre-election
- pre-eminent
- pre-empt
- pre-establish
- pre-exist
- pre-menstrual
- pre-register
- pre-wash

- prearrange
- precondition
- precook
- predate
- predispose
- prefix
- preflight
- preheat
- prehistoric
- preignition
- prejudge
- premarital
- prenatal
- preschool
- preset
- pretest
- pretrial
- prewar
- price tag
- prima-facie (adj)
- prizewinner
- prizewinning
- pro-business
- pro-labor
- pro-life
- pro-war
- profit-sharing
- pull back (v)
- pull out(v) pullout
- pullback (n)
- purebred
- push up (v)
- push-button (n
- push-up (n adj)
- put out (v)

PUNCTUATION: 199

- putout (n)
- quick-witted
- racquetball
- railroad
- railway
- rainbow
- raincheck
- raincoat
- raindrop
- rainstorm
- rainwater
- ranch house
- ranchland
- rangeland
- rank and file (n)
- rattlesnake
- rattletrap
- rawhide
- razor strop
- razzle-dazzle
- razzmatazz
- re-cover
- re-elect
- re-election
- re-emerge
- re-employ
- re-enact
- re-engage
- re-enlist
- re-enter
- re-entry
- re-equip
- re-establish
- re-examine
- re-form

- re-sign
- ready-made
- rearview mirror
- recording
- recover (regain)
- red-haired
- red-handed (adj)
- red-hot
- reform (improve)
- rendezvous
- repairman
- resign (quit)
- riffraff
- right hand (n)
- right wing (n)
- right-handed (adj)
- right-hander (n)
- right-to-work
- right-wing (adj)
- ring bearer
- rip off (v)
- rip-off (n adj)
- riverbanks
- riverboat
- roadside
- rock 'n' roll
- roll call (n)
- roll-call (adj)
- roller coaster
- roller skate (n)
- roller-skate (v)
- roly-poly
- round table (n)
- round trip (n)
- round up (v)

- round-table
- round-trip (adj)
- round-up (n)
- rubber band
- rundown
- runner-up
- running mate
- rush hour (n)
- rush-hour (adj)
- safe-deposit box
- sailboat
- sales pitch
- salesclerk
- sandbag
- sandlot
- sandstone
- sandstorm
- saucepan
- scapegoat
- scarecrow
- school bus
- schoolbook
- schoolboy
- school bus
- schoolhouse
- schoolteacher
- schoolwork
- scot-free
- seashore
- seat belt (n)
- seat-belt (adj)
- seawater
- second guess (n)
- second hand (n)
- second-guess

- second-guesser
- second-rate
- secondhand
- secretary-treasurer
- seesaw
- self-assured
- self-defense
- self-esteem
- semiannual
- semicolon
- send off (v)
- send-off (n)
- Seven-Up or 7UP
- sewer line
- shady side
- shake up (v)
- shake-up (n
- shape up (v)
- sharpshooter
- sheepskin
- Sheetrock
- ship bottom
- shirt sleeve (n)
- shirt-sleeve
- shoelace
- shoemaker
- shoeshine
- shoestring
- shoot-out (n)
- shootout (v)
- shopworn
- short-handed
- short-lived
- shortbread
- shortchange

- shotgun
- show off (v)
- showcase
- showoff
- showplace
- showroom
- showstopper
- shut down (v)
- shut in (v)
- shut off (v)
- shut-in (n)
- shut-off (n)
- shutdown (n)
- side by side (adv)
- side-by-side (adj)
- side dish
- side effect
- side street (n)
- side trip
- side-by-side
- sideburns
- sidekick
- sideshow
- sidestep
- sidetrack
- sidewalk
- sightseeing
- sightseer
- sign up (v or n)
- silversmith
- single-handed
- single-handedly
- sister-in-law
- sisterhood
- sit down (v)

- sit in (v)
- sit-down (n
- sit-in (adj n)
- sixfold
- skateboard
- skintight
- skylark
- skylight
- skyrocketing
- skyscraper
- slantwise
- slapstick
- sledgehammer
- sleight of hand (n)
- sleight-of-hand
- slide show
- slowdown
- slumlord
- slush fund
- small-arms fire
- smash up (v)
- smashup (n)
- smoke bomb
- smoke screen
- snakeskin
- snowball
- snowbank
- snowbird
- snowdrift
- snowfall
- snowflake
- snowman
- snowplow
- snowshoe
- snowstorm

- snowsuit
- so called (adv)
- soft-cover
- soft-pedal
- soft-spoken
- softball
- software
- somebody
- someday
- somehow
- someone
- someplace
- something
- sometimes
- somewhat
- somewhere
- son-in-law
- songwriter
- sound stage
- soundtrack (n)
- soundproof
- southeast
- southwest
- soybean
- space shuttle
- spacecraft
- spaceship
- spacewalk
- spearmint
- speech writer
- speech writing
- speechmaker
- speechmaking
- speed up (v)
- speedup (n adj)

- spillway
- spokesperson
- sportswear
- spot-check
- spotlight
- stagehand
- stained glass (n)
- stained-glass
- stand in (v)
- stand off (v)
- stand out (v)
- stand up (v)
- stand-in (n adj)
- stand-up (n)
- standard-bearer
- standby
- standing room
- standoff
- standoff (n adj)
- Standout
- standpipe
- standpoint
- starfish
- start up (v)
- start-up (n adj)
- state police
- statehouse
- states' rights
- statewide
- station wagon
- steamboat
- steamship
- step family
- stepbrother
- stepchild

- stepdaughter
- stepfather
- stepmother
- stepparent
- steppingstone
- stepsister
- stepson
- stockbroker
- stockroom
- stone carver
- stonewall
- stool pigeon
- stop off (v)
- stop-off (n)
- stopgap
- stoplight
- stopover
- stopwatch
- storerooms
- story line
- storyteller
- stove top (n)
- stove-top (adj)
- straight-laced
- strait-laced
- straitjacket
- street dance
- street gang
- street people
- street sweeper
- streetwise
- street-smart
- streetlamp
- streetlight
- streetwalker

- strikebreaker
- strong-willed
- stronghold
- subbasement
- subcommittee
- subculture
- subdivision
- submachine gun
- subtotal
- subway
- subzero
- summertime
- sun porch
- sunbaked
- sunbathe
- Sunday
- sundial
- sundown
- sundress
- sunfish
- sunflower
- sunglasses
- sunlit
- sunlit
- sunroof
- sunup
- supercarrier
- supercharge
- supercharge
- supercool
- superego
- superfine
- supergiant
- superhero
- superhighway

- superhuman
- superimpose
- superman
- supermarket
- supermen
- supernatural
- superpower
- superscript
- supersensitive
- supersonic
- superstar
- superstructure
- supertanker
- supertanker
- superwoman
- sweat pants
- sweatshirt
- sweetheart
- sweetmeat
- T-shirt
- table tennis
- tablecloth
- tablespoon
- tabletop
- tableware
- tadpole
- tagalong
- tail wind
- tailbone
- tailcoat
- tailgate
- taillight
- taillike
- taillike
- tailpiece

- tailspin
- take off (v)
- takeoff
- take out (v)
- take over (v)
- take up (v)
- take-home pay
- takeout (n adj)
- takeover
- talebearer
- taleteller
- tape
- tape-record (v)
- tapeworm
- taproom
- taproot
- taproot
- target
- task force
- taskmaster
- tattletale
- taxicab
- taxpayer
- teacup
- teakettle
- teammate
- teamwork
- teapot
- tear gas
- teaspoon
- teen-age (adj)
- teen-ager
- teenager
- telex (generic)
- telltale

- tenderfoot
- tenderhearted
- tenfold
- terry cloth
- textbook
- theatergoer
- themselves
- therefore
- Third World
- three R's
- throw away (v)
- throwaway
- throwback
- thumbtack
- thunderbolt
- thunderstorm
- tidbit
- tie up (v)
- tie-in (n adj)
- tie-in (v)
- tie-up (n adj)
- tiebreaker
- time sharing (n)
- time-sharing
- timekeeper
- timepieces
- timesaver
- timesaving
- timeshare
- timetable
- tiptop
- titleholder
- today
- together
- tollhouse

- Tommy gun
- toolbox
- toothpaste
- toothpick
- top-notch
- touch up (v)
- touch-up
- touchdown
- township
- toy makers
- trade in (v)
- trade off (v)
- trade-in (n adj)
- trade-off
- trademark
- trans-Atlantic
- trans-Pacific
- transcontinental
- transmigrate
- transoceanic
- transsexual
- transship '
- trash can
- trendsetter
- trigger-happy
- truck driver
- truck stop
- try out
- tryout (n)
- tune up (v)
- tuneup (n adj)
- turboprop
- turn off (v)
- turnabout
- turnaround

- turnbuckle
- turncoat
- turndown
- turnkey
- turnoff
- turnpike
- turntable
- twofold
- typewriter
- U-boat
- U-turn
- ultramodern
- ultrasonic
- ultraviolet
- un-American
- unarmed
- underway
- underachieve
- underact
- underage
- underarm
- underbelly
- underbid
- undercharge
- underclothes
- undercover
- undercurrent
- undercut
- underdog
- underestimate
- underexpose
- underfoot
- underground
- undersheriff
- undersold

- up-tempo
- upbeat
- upbringing
- upcoming
- update
- upend
- upgrade
- upheaval
- upheld
- uphill
- uphold
- upkeep
- upland
- uplift
- uplink
- upload
- upmarket
- upon
- upper hand
- uppercase
- upperclassman
- uppercut
- uppermost
- upright
- uprising
- uproar
- uproot
- upscale
- upset
- upshot
- upside
- upside down (adv)
- upside-down
- upstage
- upstairs

- upstanding
- upstart
- upstate
- upstate
- upstream
- upstroke
- uptake
- upthrust
- uptight
- uptime
- uptown
- upturn
- upward
- upwind
- V-8
- V-J Day
- V-neck
- vice chancellor
- vice consul
- vice president
- vice principal
- vice regent
- vice secretary
- vice versa
- video game
- videocassette (n adj)
- videodisc
- videotape (n v)
- voodoo
- vote-getter
- wagon master
- wagonmaker
- waistline
- walk on (v)
- walk up (v)

- walk-on (n)
- walk-up (n adj)
- walkways
- wall covering
- wall hanging
- walleyed
- wallpaper
- war horse (horse)
- wardroom
- warehouse
- warfare
- warhead
- warhorse (veteran)
- warlike
- warlord
- warm-up
- warm-blooded
- warmhearted
- warning
- warpath
- wartime
- wash out (v)
- washboard
- washbowl
- washcloth
- washed up (v)
- washed-up (adj)
- washhouse
- washout
- washout (n)
- washrag
- washroom
- washstand
- washtub
- waste water

- wastebasket
- wasteland
- wastepaper
- wastewater
- watch
- watchband
- watchdog
- watchmaker
- watchman
- watchtower
- watchword
- water bed
- water ski (n)
- water tank
- water-ski (v)
- water-skiing
- watercolor
- watercooler
- watercraft
- waterfall
- waterfowl
- waterfront
- waterline
- waterline
- waterlog
- watermark
- watermelon
- waterpower
- waterproof
- waterscape
- watershed
- waterside
- waterspout
- watertight
- waterway

- waterwheel
- waterworks
- wavelength
- wavelike
- waxwork
- waybill
- wayfarer
- waylaid
- wayside
- wayward
- weak-kneed
- weather vane
- weather-beaten
- weathercock
- weatherman
- weatherproof
- week-nights
- weekday
- weekend
- weeklong
- weeknight
- weightlifting
- well-being
- well-to-do
- well-wishers
- wet bar
- whatever
- whatsoever
- wheelbarrow
- wheelbase
- wheelchair
- wheeler-dealer
- wheelhouse
- whereabouts
- wherever

- whirlwind
- white collar (n) white-collar (adj)
- white paper
- white water (n)
- white-water (adj)
- whitecap
- whitefish
- whitewall
- whitewash
- whole-wheat
- wholehearted
- wholesale price index
- wide-angle
- wide-awake
- wide-eyed
- wide-open
- wide.-brimmed
- widespread
- wifebeater
- willpower
- windchill index
- wind power
- wind up (v)
- wind-swept
- window-dress (v)
- window-shop (v)
- window-shop-
- wine taster
- winemaking
- wingspan
- winter storm
- wintertime
- wipeout
- wiretap
- without

- wood heat
- wood-burning
- woodcarver
- woodcarving
- woodshop
- woodsmoke
- woodstove
- woodwork
- word-of-mouth
- work force
- workday
- working class (n)
- working-class
- workout
- workplace
- workweek
- worldwide
- worn-out
- write in (v)
- write-in (n adj)
- wrongdoing
- X-ray
- yard sale
- year-end (adj)
- year-round
- yearlong
- yesteryear
- yo-yo
- yuletide
- zigzag

This is not a comprehensive list. In order to get all the words, I'll need your help, so send in suggestions of any that are missing.

But no matter how you look at it, it's a hell of a good start. If you make a few text shortcuts using a text expansion app like I described in *No Mistakes Writing Volume I—Writing Shortcuts,* you'll have access to this list within seconds. That way, if you have doubts about which form to use, hit the keystroke that pulls up the list, then simply do a quick search for the word you're looking for.

Also, as always, if in doubt, consult a dictionary. Example—one of the words on this list—*archrival*—my spellchecker insists is wrong, but when you check it with *Merriam-Webster's*, it shows it as spelled correctly. *Oxford English Dictionary*, however, lists it as *arch-rival*, with a hyphen.

One more example of why you need to consult a dictionary.

Note:

One thought is that if your favorite writing app has a spellchecker you like, use it to *learn* the words you have issues with. For example, if it flags a word like *archrival* as being inaccurate, and you know it's right, add it to the spellchecker's corpus so it won't flag it again.

I've had to do this with numerous words, but it's a good way to conform to the dictionary you want to use.

Chapter Seventeen
EN AND EM DASHES

En Dashes and Em Dashes and How to Use Them

We recently discussed hyphens, so it may be a good time to go over en dashes and em dashes. After all, they're kind of the same, right?

Not really.

They may look similar, but they have different functions and different rules regarding when and how to use them, not to mention how to type them on a keyboard.

Hyphens, en Dashes, Em Dashes

To understand dashes and how they're used to punctuate sentences, it's important to grasp what they're used for and, just as importantly, what they're *not* used for. I'm going to let CMOS (*Chicago Manual of Style*) do that, though I may remove some of their grammatical terms and two-dollar words. All three of the following definitions came from *Chicago*.

Hyphen

> The hyphen connects two things that are closely related, usually words that work together as a single concept or work together as a joint modifier (e.g., tie-in, toll-free call, two-thirds).

En dash

: The en dash connects things that are related to each other by distance, as in the May–September issue of a magazine; or the dates of employment on a résumé, such as 2002–2015; or even a range of pages in a book, 155–193.

Em dash

The em dash allows, in a manner similar to parentheses, an additional thought to be added within a sentence by sort of breaking away from that sentence.

: 1B. Em dashes also substitute for something missing.

: 1C. Also, the em dash may serve as a sort of bullet point.

Note: In all instances, you don't use spaces on either side of any dashes (hyphens included), although that is *Chicago's* recommendation. Some style books may disagree. Below is a screenshot comparing the relative sizes of hyphens, en dashes, and em dashes. Below the dashes are the letters *I, n,* and *m* to show the approximate size.

Hyphen, en dash, em dash

En Dashes and Labeling Times

In almost any form of business writing or, for that matter, any form of writing, you will find it necessary to list a time, or times, in the communication. Here is the proper way to do it:

- The interviews will be conducted between 8:00 and 4:00.

You would not say "The interviews will be conducted between 8:00–4:00."

If you use the words *between* or *from*, you do not use an en dash; however, if you do not use either of those words, an en dash is not only fine but required.

- The interviews will be conducted 8:00–4:00.

This rule isn't followed often, but it is a rule. If you want to look as if you know your grammar, stick to it.

An en dash is longer than a hyphen and shorter than an em dash. The en dash's name derives from the fact that it is approximately the same width as the letter *N*.

Another point about en dashes is whenever you would say the words *to* or *through* where the dash is, it is likely an en dash that's needed, not a hyphen or em dash. Examples follow:

✗ He was a hands-on manager. (hyphen)

✗ It wasn't him—it was her! (em dash)

✓ I took the Houston–Philly–Boston flight. (en dash)

✓ Director of Sales, 1994–2017. (en dash)

✓ We travel to Europe every year, usually May–August (en dash).

Notice that in each situation where we used the en dash (green checked sentences) you could have substituted the word *to* or *through* and it would have sounded right.

- I took the Houston *to* Philly *to* Boston flight.
- Director of Sales, 1994 *to/through* 2017.
- We travel to Europe every year, usually May *to/through* August.

There is something to be aware of, though (as discussed above). If you use the words *from* or *between* to introduce a phrase that would ordinarily contain an en dash, you need to use the words *to* or *and* (respectively) instead of the en dash. Let's use the above sentences as examples. (Some rewording may be necessary to be grammatically correct.)

✓ I took the flight *from* Houston *to* Philly *to* Boston.

✓ Director of Sales *from* 1994 *to/through* 2017.

✓ We travel to Europe every year, usually *from* May *to/through* August.

✗ I took the flight *from* Houston–Philly–Boston.

✗ Director of Sales, *from* 1994–2017

✘ We travel to Europe every year, usually *from* May–August.
✓ He smokes *between* two *and* three packs of cigarettes per day.
✓ She takes the connecting train *between* Rome *and* Naples every night.
✘ He smokes *between* two–three packs of cigarettes per day.
✘ She takes the connecting train *between* Rome–Naples every night.
✓ The Yankees beat the Red Sox 6–2 (six *to* two) last night.
✓ The Philly–NY (Philly *to* NY) train ride only takes ninety minutes.

We mentioned earlier that you don't use spaces on either side of a dash, but some style guides suggest you do. CMOS recommends no spaces before or after a dash, so it would look like this:

- . . . it's him—not her.

AP recommends spaces around dashes, but their recommended dictionary (Webster's New World College Dictionary), does not. Their recommended style looks like this:

- . . . it's him — not her.

Some style guides, including a lot of British ones, recommend using the en dash *with* spaces instead of the em dash, so the same sentence we listed first, it would look like this:

- . . . it's him – not her.

You may also use en dashes to refer to an "open-ended date"; that is, an unfinished date range (where the closing date has not been established), as would be the case when citing the range of years someone has been alive when they haven't died yet. Or the publication date for a magazine still in circulation. Examples follow:

- Robert De Niro (1943–)

- Steven Spielberg (1946–)
- Sports Illustrated (1954–)

Sometimes an en dash is used to denote different places for universities (or companies, etc.) that have more than one location. The examples below show how it's written using en dashes.

- The University of California–San Diego
- The University of Texas–Austin
- Texas A&M University–College Station

That's not the only way such locations may be listed, though, so check to make sure beforehand. Commas could be used just as efficiently.

- The University of California, San Diego
- The University of Texas, Austin
- Texas A&M University, College Station

The institutions may also choose to simply use words:

- The University of California at San Diego
- The University of Texas at Austin
- Texas A&M University at College Station

That sums up en dashes. Now on to the en dash's big brother—the em dash.

The Most Common Use of Em Dashes

For clarification, here are a few real-life examples of the three *primary* functions of an em dash.

1. To take the place of a colon, but with more punch.

Carla hated three things—deception, falsehoods, and lies.

Notice how that one piece of punctuation adds emphasis to the sentence. Yes, the words helped, but a colon wouldn't have been the same.

✻ Carla hated three things: deception, falsehoods, and lies.

I don't know about you, but I can almost *feel* the disgust in the first example, and the second is pretty bland, as if she's citing a list of things she needs at the grocery store.

2. To offset a parenthetical phrase or thought.

✻ No matter what happened—good, bad, or indifferent—in Uncle Dominic's house it was cause to put espresso on the stove.

3. To indicate an interruption in dialogue.

✻ "I'm through talking," he said. "The next time—"

✻ "There won't be a 'next time,'" she said, and slammed the door.

Note

I know there should be no comma following *said* in the sentence above (repeated below):

- "There won't be a 'next time,'" she said, and slammed the door.

I didn't use the comma because it's the way I punctuate dialogue, and I like it. I explain it in one of my books: *Editing Made Easy*.

Don't think the examples above are the only uses of the em dash; there are many more. Along with the above reasons, there are other situations where you may see em dashes used frequently:

- To introduce a phrase or clause that summarizes what has just been said.

✻ Exercising, drinking a lot of water, and throwing away your cigarettes—these are three simple things to keep you healthy.

✻ To introduce several expressions, such as "that is," "namely," and "for example." As usual, examples follow:

- "My husband loves most working dogs—namely, Australian shepherds, Australian cattle dogs, and Anatolian shepherds."
- "I used to breed fish, and I loved the aggressive ones—for example, African and South American cichlids."
- During World War I, the Ottoman Empire and Hungary fought against the Allies—that is, they fought with the Germans.

One thing to note in the sentences above is that commas would normally precede *namely*, *that is*, and *for example*; however, you *do not* precede an em dash with a comma. The em dash serves in place of the comma. Under certain circumstances, it's acceptable to use an exclamation point or a question mark, and you may use a period if it concludes with an abbreviation. You also don't use semicolons or colons immediately preceding an em dash.

- For no reason he left—was he warned?—and he took his gun with him.
- The only reason for you to drive—God forbid!—is if everyone else is drunk.
- He insists on being addressed by his full title—Dr. Milton Abrams, M.D.—and we must abide if we want him to stay.

In the cases above, note the use of the punctuation preceding the em dash. It's rare you'd see this construction, but if you run across examples like the above, this is how to punctuate them.

One more thing about em dashes is that in special circumstances they may be used in place of a word. It may be a curse word you don't want to list, or it may be the name of someone you want to keep confidential.

In circumstances such as this (when an em dash is used in place of one or more words), use two or three em dashes to let the readers know (just be consistent).

- The foreman of the jury——read the guilty verdict today

at 11:00 a.m. (The em dashes represent the foreman's name).
- The young woman——was attacked and raped just before midnight while on her way home (same thing).
- When the foreman read the verdict, the defendant, noted mobster Carlo Giannini became vocal. "I'll kill you for this, you——rat. You're dead meat." (The em dashes are in place of the foul language he used.)

Bottom Line

To neatly wrap up dashes:

- A hyphen is used to connect compound modifiers (among other things), such as "hands-on manager," and "high-volume manufacturing."
- An en dash is used to show a range of dates (among other things), such as "2003–Present."
- An em dash might be used in a cover letter for a job application, such as this: "As general manager—and temporary vice president of sales—drove profits to record levels."

One more note about em dashes—they are often used in regular prose to add a little punch. I'll give you an example.

Imagine you're writing a scene where a family is having dinner at a restaurant someone's recommended. Let's imagine the maître d' approaches the table and asks how things are going. You might write the following:

- We ordered dinner an hour ago, and it hasn't arrived yet.

But if you wanted it to carry more punch, you might write:

- We ordered dinner—about an hour ago—and it hasn't arrived yet.

I don't know about you, but I think the second example carries more emphasis.

Technical Details

- To make hyphen (-), press the hyphen key on the keyboard.
- To make an en dash (–), press *option-* on a Mac or *control* and *minus sign* on the numeric keypad.
- To make an em dash (—), press *option/shift/hyphen* on a Mac or *control/alt* and *minus* key on the numeric keypad of a PC.

Chapter Eighteen
QUIZ 7

Quiz 7

This quiz is for *you* to punctuate. Each sentence deals with subject-verb agreement.

- Bob and his dog (do/does) everything together.
- My mom, as well as my dad, (are/is) going to the party.
- (There's/there are) a lot to do before we're done.
- He, my sister, and my dad (jog/jogs) every morning.

Chapter Nineteen
QUIZ 8

Quiz 8 (Select the sentences that are correct.)

He said he'd go to the theater. (Will he?)
   He said he'd go to the theater. (will he?)
   He said he'd go to the theater (Will he?).
   He said he'd go to the theater (will he?).
   He said he'd go to the theater. (Will he?).

"She said (at least, I think she said), 'Let's go to the beach.' "
   "She said (at least I think she said), 'Let's go to the beach.' "
   "She said (at least, I think she said), "Let's go to the beach."
   "She said, (at least, I think she said), 'Let's go to the beach.' "

We saw a koala bear (have you ever seen one?) when we went to the zoo.
   We saw a koala bear, (have you ever seen one?) when we went to the zoo.

We saw a koala bear, (Have you ever seen one?) when we went to the zoo.

We saw a koala bear (Have you ever seen one?), when we went to the zoo.

We saw a koala bear (have you ever seen one?) when we went to the zoo.

Chapter Twenty
SLASHES

The forward slash (/) is not recommended for formal writing; however, it is used frequently with informal writing. Here are a few examples of how it's used.

Perhaps the most frequently seen usage is for fractions or dates, as the first few examples show.

- ½
- 11/17/16

It is also used in place of *or* in some cases.

- He/she was the one who robbed me.

A slash may also be used with abbreviations:

- w/o [for without]
- c/o [*for* care of]
- w/w [*for* wall-to-wall]

And from the *Merriam-Webster's Manual for Writers and Editors*:

If the letter is being used to refer to its sound and not its printed form, slashes or brackets are used instead of italics in technical contexts.

>The pure /p/ sound is rarely heard in the mountain dialect.

— MERRIAM-WEBSTER'S

You may think this is an extremely rare case, but it's not. For people who deal with teaching phonics by the sounds letters make (phonemes), it is an everyday practice.

If you ever browsed a dictionary or looked up a word you didn't know how to pronounce, invariably, phonemes were used to sound it out. I've shown *through, cow,* and others below as they are listed by *Merriam-Webster's*. (I removed the parts of speech designation so it didn't confuse anyone.)

- through: \'thrü\
- cow: \'kaù\
- fan·tas·tic: \fan-'ta-stik, fən-\
- cat: \'kat\
- pho·neme: \'fō-,nēm\

By the way, the above examples are the only times I know of other than computer programming, where a backslash (\ ) is used on a regular basis.

The "vertical slash" or "upright slash" (|) is used in mathematical expressions and computer programming.

ACKNOWLEDGMENTS

This book wouldn't have been as complete or as good without the help of Jeanne Haskin and JJ. Toner who provided a tremendous amount of feedback and valuable suggestions as well as correcting many mistakes.

I also need to thank my four grandkids, Joey, Dante, Adalina, and Carmine, who provide endless inspiration and undying support.

I also need to thank my editor, Michele Preisendorf, of Eschler Editing, for her undying patience and diligence in keeping me straight.

ABOUT THE AUTHOR

Giacomo Giammatteo is the author of gritty crime dramas about murder, mystery, and family. He also writes non-fiction books including the No Mistakes Careers series, No Mistakes Publishing, No Mistakes Grammar, and No Mistakes Writing.

When Giacomo isn't writing, he's helping his wife take care of the animals on their sanctuary. At last count, they had forty-five animals—eleven dogs, a horse, six cats, and twenty-six pigs.

Oh, and one crazy—and very large—wild boar, who takes walks with Giacomo every day and also happens to be his best buddy.

nomistakespublishing.com
gg@giacomog.com

ALSO BY GIACOMO GIAMMATTEO

You can see all of my books here.
And you can buy them on the platform of your choice.

This brings up a thought: with more than fifty books out now, it is becoming difficult to try to update the list in the back of all of them. If you want to know what books I have out, use the link above, which takes you to my website, or download the latest copy of my GG recommended reading list, which is free.

Nonfiction :

Careers:

No Mistakes Resumes, Book I of No Mistakes Careers

No Mistakes Interviews, Book II of No Mistakes Careers

Grammar:

Misused Words, No Mistakes Grammar, Volume I

Misused Words for Business, No Mistakes Grammar, Volume II

More Misused Words, No Mistakes Grammar, Volume III

Visual Grammar (this is a compilation of volumes I–III with a bit of new information added. It also includes pictures. The world's first visual grammar book)

Misused Words and Then Some, No Mistakes Grammar, Volume V

More Grammar:

No Mistakes Grammar Bites, Volume I, Lie, Lay, Laid, and It's and Its

No Mistakes Grammar Bites, Volume II, Good and Well, and Then and Than

No Mistakes Grammar Bites, Volume III, That, Which, and Who, and There Is and There Are

No Mistakes Grammar Bites, Volume IV, Affect and Effect, and Accept and Except

No Mistakes Grammar Bites, Volume V, You're and Your, and They're, There, and Their

No Mistakes Grammar Bites, Volume VI, Passed and Past, and Into, In To and In

No Mistakes Grammar Bites, Volume VII, Farther and Further, and Onto, On, and On To

No Mistakes Grammar Bites, Volume VIII, Anxious and Eager, and Different From and Different Than

No Mistakes Grammar Bites, Volume IX, A While and Awhile, and Envy and Jealousy

No Mistakes Grammar Bites, Volume X, Could've and Should've, and Irony and Coincidence

No Mistakes Grammar Bites, Volume XI, "Quotation Marks and How to Punctuate Them" and "Plurals of Compound Nouns"

No Mistakes Grammar Bites, Volume XII, "Latin Abbreviations

No Mistakes Grammar Bites, Volume XIII, "Redundancies" and "Ax to Grind"

No Mistakes Grammar Bites Volume XIV, "Superlatives and How We Use them Wrong"

No Mistakes Grammar Bites Volume XV, "Shoo-in and Shoe-in" and "Horse Racing Sayings"

No Mistakes Grammar Bites Volume XVI, "Which and What" and "Since and Because"

No Mistakes Grammar Bites Volume XVII, "Hyphens, and When to Use Them" and "Em Dashes and En Dashes"

No Mistakes Grammar Bites Volume XVIII, "Words Difficult to Pronounce" and "Could Not Care Less"

No Mistakes Grammar Bites Volume XIX, "Punctuation" and "When You Don't Need the Word Personal"

No Mistakes Grammar Bites, Volume XX, "When Is Currently Needed?" And "Intervene and Interfere"

No Mistakes Grammar Bites, Volume XXI, "More Hyphen Questions" and Myself, Me, Themselves and Themselves."

No Mistakes Grammar Bites, Volume XXII, "Words You May Be Using Wrong, Part One"

No Mistakes Grammar Bites, Volume XXIII, Words You May Be Using Wong, Part II

No Mistakes Grammar Bites, Volume XXIV, "If and Whether," and "Incredible"

No Mistakes Grammar Bites, Volume XXV, "Use or Utilize" and "Dilemma"

No Mistakes Grammar Bites, Volume XXVI, "Alternate and Alternative" and "Plethora"

Writing:

No Mistakes Writing, Volume I—Writing Shortcuts

No Mistakes Writing, Volume II—How to Write a Bestseller

No Mistakes Writing, Volume III—Editing Made Easy

No Mistakes Writing, Volume IV—Writing Rules for Writers Who Don't Like Rules (coming soon)

Publishing:

How to Publish an eBook, No Mistakes Publishing, Volume I

How to Format an eBook, No Mistakes Publishing, Volume II

eBook Distribution, No Mistakes Publishing, Volume III

Print on Demand—Who to Use to Print Your Books, No Mistakes Publishing, Volume IV

Other nonfiction

Uneducated

Whiskers and Bear—Volume I, Sanctuary Tales

A Collection of Animal Stories, Volume II, Sanctuary Tales

More Animal Stories, Volume III, Sanctuary Tales Surviving a Stroke—or Two

Life and Then Some

Fiction:

Friendship & Honor Series:

Murder Takes Time

Murder Has Consequences

Murder Takes Patience

Murder Is Invisible

Murder Is a Promise

Murder Is Immaculate (coming soon)

Blood Flows South Series:

A Bullet For Carlos: A Connie Gianelli Mystery

Finding Family, a Novella

A Bullet From Dominic

The Good Book

The Ranger (coming soon)

Redemption Series:

Necessary Decisions: A Gino Cataldi Mystery

Old Wounds

Promises Kept, the Story of Number Two

Premeditated

The Ranger (coming soon)

Rules of Vengeance Series: (Fantasy)

Light of Lights (the beginning, a novella)

A Promise of Vengeance

Undeniable Vengeance

Consummate Vengeance

Vengeance Is Mine (2019)

Note. The Light of Lights is a novella. It's about 100 pages long and sets the stage for the series. The other books in the series are between 650 and 850 pages long.

OTHER BOOKS

You can always see the current and coming-soon books on my website.

Fiction:

Memories for Sale **(mystery/sf)**

The Joshua Citadel **(SF novella)**

Children's Books:

No Mistakes Grammar for Kids, Volume I—Much and Many

No Mistakes Grammar for Kids, Volume II—Lie and Lay

No Mistakes Grammar for Kids, Volume III—Bring and Take

No Mistakes Grammar for Kids, Volume IV, "Would've, Should've" and "Your and You're"

No Mistakes Grammar for Kids, Volume V, "There, They're, and Their" and "To, Too, and Two"

Shinobi Goes to School—Life on the Farm for Kids, Volume I

Fiona Gets Caught, Life on the Farm for Kids, Volume II

Coco Gets a Donut, Life on the Farm for Kids, Volume III

Squeak Gets a Home, Life on the Farm for Kids, Volume IV

Biscotti Saves Punch, Life on the Farm for Kids, Volume V

The Adventures of Adalina, Volume I, Adalina and the Five Tiny Bears

Coming Soon:

The Adventures of Adalina, Volume II, Adalina and the Underwater Bears

Get on the mailing list, and you'll be sure to be notified of release dates and sales.

[Mailing list](#)

And don't forget to leave a review!

Part Two
HOW TO PUNCTUATE DIALOGE

This is not advice on creating good dialogue. This section deals with the specifics of how to punctuate dialogue. A later chapter deals with how to capitalize dialogue.

Chapter Twenty-One
PUNCTUATING DIALOGUE

How to Punctuate Dialogue

I've written about dialogue several times: how to capitalize it and how to use dialogue tags. Today, we'll talk about how to properly punctuate it.

Many writers will tell you that writing realistic dialogue is one of the bigger challenges when putting together a novel. It's difficult to make the dialogue sound realistic without boring the readers. Part of the trick to doing it right is to ensure it is punctuated properly.

As I've said many times, punctuation is critical to a comfortable and enjoyable read.

Dialogue is critical to a good novel. It not only moves your plot along, it is one of the bigger factors in developing character, which, in my opinion, is key to a good novel.

How do you punctuate dialogue? It's both easier and more difficult than you may think.

Dialogue consists of the words that a character speaks, and those words are always enclosed in quotations. The words need to be spoken aloud, but even if they're whispered or mumbled, the quotations are needed.

- "You can't go to the party," Sean's father said.
- Sean's father said, "You can't go to the party."

If one of your characters is simply thinking something, use italics to designate that.

- *I shouldn't let him go to the party*, Sean's father thought.

If you want to get rid of the "Sean's father thought" part, try using a beat first to clue the reader as to who's speaking.

- Sean's father got up from the chair and paced. *I shouldn't let him go to the party.*

We'll discuss capitalizing dialogue in the chapter dealing with capitalization; instead, let's concentrate on the other punctuation.

Going back to the first example, notice the punctuation following "party" is *inside* the quotation marks. Remember, periods and commas *always* go inside the quotation marks in American English (with almost no exceptions).

Also note in the second sentence there is a comma following "said." That's because it introduces a direct quotation—Sean's father saying "You can't go to the party."

- Sean sulked for a moment, then said, "I don't care what you said. I'm going!"
- His father glared. "What did you say, young man?"

In the two examples above, the exclamation point and the question mark were also inside the quotation marks because they were part of the sentences.

Dialogue Interrupted, and Then Continued by the Same Speaker

- As Sean left the room, his father slammed his fist on the

table and said, "I'll tell you what I should have done . . ." He took a few deep breaths and a sip of wine. "I should have grounded his ass."

No matter if dialogue is continued by the same speaker (as above) or by someone else, the quotation marks are used as they always are.

Whenever you are addressing someone directly, use a comma before their name even if it's a nickname (though not a term of endearment).

- "Sean, you'll do *what* I say, and you'll do it *when* I say it."
- Sean mock-saluted his father, then went to his room. His brother was watching TV and looked over when Sean came in.
- "I heard you and Dad arguing. What did he say?"
- "He said, 'You'll do *what* I say, and you'll do it *when* I say it.'"

Let's analyze this exchange of dialogue and see why it was punctuated the way it was.

- "Sean, you'll do *what* I say, and you'll do it *when* I say it."

This one is easy, the entire quote is in quotations. "Sean" is offset with a comma because he is being spoken to. There is a comma after "say" because the punctuation is following the rules for sentences using *connecting* words (and) when followed by independent clauses. (you'll do it when I say it.) And the period at the end is *inside* the quotation marks because that's where periods go.

- Sean mock-saluted his father, then went to his room. His brother was watching TV and looked over when Sean came in.
- "I heard you and Dad arguing. What did he say?"

- "He said, 'You'll do *what* I say, and you'll do it *when* I say it.' "

Sentence two and three should be self-explanatory. In sentence three, "Dad" was capitalized. The chapter dealing with capitalization of dialogue will explain that.

Sentence four is full of things to analyze. The sentence is surrounded by quotation marks, and the comma after "He said" is there because it is introducing an indirect quote. (Sean is telling his brother what his father said, word for word.) "You'll" is preceded by a single quotation mark because that's what you do with a quote within a quote (at least in American English). The comma after "say" is the same as in sentence one, as is the period.

The single quotation mark after "it" closes out the indirect quote. There is a *half space* following the single quotation mark and before the double quotation mark.

That took up a lot of space, but I hope it was clear.

Nicknames

- "Mom, is there any cake left?"
- "You know what I said, young man. No cake until we get to Uncle Bob's."

In the sentences above, notice that a comma follows "Mom" even though it's not her true name. It also precedes "young man."

Dialogue That Continues for More Than One Paragraph

When you have a long passage of dialogue, and it continues for more than one paragraph, you do not use closing quotation marks on the first paragraph, but you do open the second with quotation marks. Below is an example.

Detective Cinalli paced, frustrated with his officer's action. "You can't pass judgment on someone because you *think* he's guilty.

"It's not right, and it's against the law. I don't want to hear of anything like this again. Understood?"

There are a few things that a writer can change and attribute it to a style choice, but it would be wise to conform to what are considered the accepted rules.

No matter what though, be consistent.

Summary

We covered the placement of semicolons, colons, and em dashes with quotation marks in an earlier chapter, so let's move on to punctuating dialogue tags.

Chapter Twenty-Two
PUNCTUATING DIALOGUE TAGS

Good dialogue is key to an enjoyable book, and proper punctuation is key to good dialogue.

I've mentioned previously that I don't believe in writing rules. I view "writing rules" and even grammar rules as guidelines. The grammar ones I adhere to almost all the time, but that may be because I agree with them.

There is one grammar rule that I am not such a staunch supporter of though, and we'll discuss that now.

This is a rule we've already discussed in the chapter on commas. It is implied as part of "rule number two."

> Use a comma before a coordinating conjunction that connects two independent clauses.

The flip side of this rule is that you *do not* use a comma if a coordinating conjunction (connecting word) is used to connect clauses other than independent ones. Following that rule, in the following sentences, the first *would not* require a comma and the second one would.

- She went to the bank and made a deposit.
- She went to the bank, and she made a deposit.

To me, commas imply a sequence of events:

- Honey, would you please stop at the hardware store, pick up our prescriptions, and get some milk.

That request indicates a sequence in the actions that need to be performed. She wants him to go to the hardware store, pick up the prescriptions, and *then* stop and get milk.

The example consists of three things in the list, so it needs commas; however, even if it had only two things, I feel it would be better with a comma.

- Honey, would you pick up a hammer while you're out, and get a gallon of milk, please.

When I read this, I can picture the husband stopping to get the hammer and then stopping to get the milk. And when things like this occur with dialogue, it seems like even more of a sequence. Look at the following.

- "I'm not staying here any longer!" she said and slammed the door.

This is the way the above sentence *should* be punctuated. But I view the sentence written that way as a woman standing with the door half open and shouting that she isn't staying there any longer.

I prefer to use a comma in cases like this, especially if I'm trying to convey a different sequence of events.

- "I'm not staying here any longer!" she said, and slammed the door.

When I read the same sentence *with* a comma, I picture her making the statement (possibly even in another room), and *then* slamming the door as she left.

I realize I could have easily said, "and then" or even "then," but there are times when I don't want to use that construction so often.

My solution to this is simple. I use a comma in cases where an example like that occurs within a dialogue tag, and I adhere to the rules when it doesn't, such as the example with the bank deposit. The main thing is I do it consistently.

Chapter One
HALF SPACES OR THIN SPACES

Half spaces

What they're used for and how to make them.

Before we start, I need to let you know this advice is for people who own a Mac. There's a workaround for PCs, and I'm sure there's a way to make a thin space naturally on a PC, but I don't use a PC, so I don't know the details.

If you own a PC and can't find a way to do it, you can get someone with a Mac to email the half space to you. If you don't know someone with a Mac, email me.

I suppose I should explain what a thin space is and when and why you need to use one.

One of the only times you use single quotation marks in American English is when you cite a quote within a quote:

- Jim said, "Mom's exact words were 'Tell him to come home now.' "

The entire sentence had to be put in quotation marks, and the "Tell him to come home now," had to be in single quotes because those are the words his mother spoke. That's using a quote within a quote. The problem comes at the end of the sentence.

Typographical rules say there should be a small space between the single and double quotation marks. A regular space is too wide, so you're supposed to use what's called a "thin space" or a "half space." The problem is that most people don't know how to make one.

I searched for days. I even called Apple, but no one could tell me how to make a "thin space." Then I ran across an article written by Steve Sande from AppleWorld Today. I wrote him, and he graciously responded with instructions on how to make a thin space. I'll share that with you. (By the way, that is a thin space separating the quotation marks above.)

Getting Ready

Remember, these instructions are only for a Mac, and know that you can't type this in from the keyboard. You'll need to open "Systems Preferences" > "Keyboard" > "Input Sources" and check the box that says "Show input menu in menu bar."

The menu bar will offer two choices: "Show emoji and symbols" and "Show Keyboard Viewer." Select "Show Emoji and Symbols," which brings up the Character Viewer. It should look something like this:

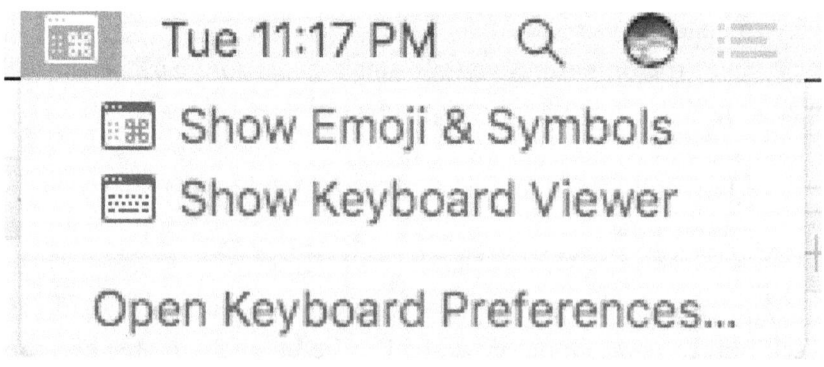

Now click on "Show Emoji and Symbols" and it will open up a window similar to the image below.

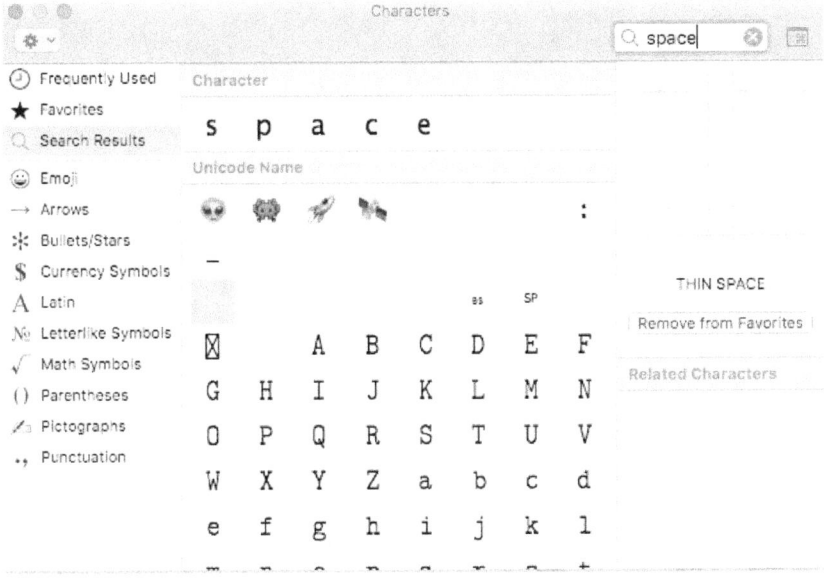

Type "space" in the top right search bar and you should be rewarded with an image that looks like the above. Notice the highlighted item on the far left, third row down. If you look to the right side of the image, you'll see it lists it as a "thin space."

This is the item you want. Click to add it to "Favorites." You'll notice my window says, "Remove from Favorites," but that's because I already added it.

Once you add the thin space to your favorites, click on "Favorites." It won't look like this because this is showing how mine looks, displaying the favorites I have chosen, but it will show the highlighted "thin space." To insert the space into your document, place the cursor where you want the space to go, then double-click.

You may think, "That's a lot of trouble to go through for a space," but there are ways around that.

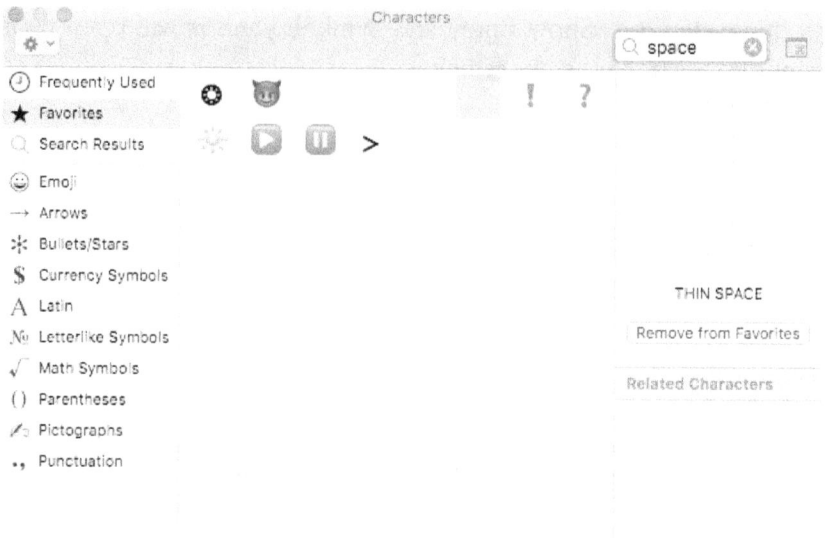

The first is a simple solution that will save you time. Much of the time, you'll encounter the need for a thin space when quoting someone else, which often happens in books or long documents.

Write the entire project without using thin spaces, then, when you're done, use the "Find and Replace" function to search for every situation where there is a single quote (') next to a double quote ("). It should look something like this: ('"). Now replace the single and double quotes with a single quote, thin space, and double quote.

This method is a lot easier than having to deal with the keyboard viewer for every occurrence, but it's still not ideal. Let's look at a few other ways to handle it.

The easiest way, in my opinion, is to use a text-expansion program. I use one called Text Expander™. You can check it out here:

This may also be a way for people with PCs to use a "thin space" as Text Expander™ makes a PC version.

If that's an acceptable option, find a way to copy the space from a Mac. (The easiest way I can think of is to have someone with a

Mac email it to you.) Once you have the thin space, copy it to your text-expansion program and you'll have it permanently.

Once it's in your text-expansion program, assign it a shortcut you'll remember. I gave mine a simple one: "thinspace," with no space between *thin* and *space*, and I set it to expand immediately. You could also assign it something like "halfspace" or anything you'll remember easily.

Text Expander makes it so easy to do almost anything faster that I even wrote a book about it: *Writing Shortcuts.*

Option number two makes things easy as well, and that is using an app called "Paste" that allows you to have unlimited copy and paste functions, and it's as simple as using ⌘, ⇧, and *v* simultaneously. Below is a screenshot.

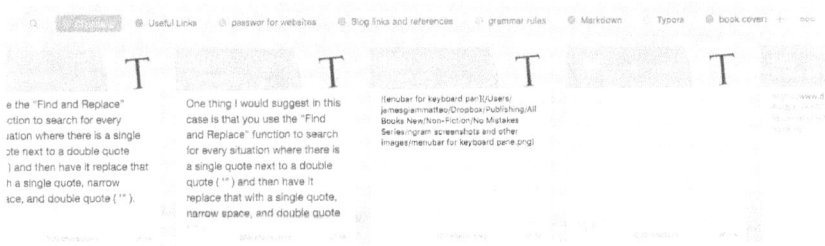

Each new item you copy will show up on the left. There are also places to store an item permanently as shown above in the areas marked with red and green dots. I have my "thin space" stored with other things I may find a need for like ! ? and many more.

So there you have it: a way to type a "thin space" as well as three alternatives, and even a way for those with a PC to do it (assuming they know someone with a Mac who is willing to share the *thin space* with them).

Now that I've put you through all this, I have found a way to make a thin space in Microsoft Word. And it's not difficult.

Type any sentence, then highlight a space between two words only. If you want to have a copy of the single quote/thin space/double quote, then type that using a full space. It should look like this: ' ".

Highlight the space portion only, not the quotes.

If you're using a PC, type "Control D" (^ D). On a Mac, type "Command D" (⌘ D). It will bring up a dialogue box similar to the one below. (This is from a Mac.)

```
                              Font
                        Font    Advanced

Character Spacing
              Scale:  100%
            Spacing:  Normal        By:
           Position:  Normal        By:
    Kerning for fonts:          Points and above

Advanced Typography
          Ligatures:  None
     Number spacing:  Default
       Number forms:  Default
      Stylistic sets:  Default
      Use contextual alternates
   ☑ Enable TrueType typography features

Preview
   _____         , "         _____

   Default...                         Cancel    OK
```

Go to the "Advanced" tab up top and then access the "Scale" dropdown menu (It will initially show 100%). Set it to the scale you want. Fifty percent is recommended for this.

That's it; you're done. This would be a chore to do every time, so if you don't have a text expansion app or an app like *Paste*, create a new *Word* document and make your '" the only thing in the document, then put it somewhere that it's easy to access so you can copy and paste.

Part Three
ANSWERS TO QUIZZES

The quizzes dealt mainly with punctuation issues that were covered in the first section. One dealt with subject-verb agreement.

Chapter Twenty-Three
ANSWERS TO QUIZ 1

Answers To Quiz One

1. ✗ Sally went home for a nap then decided to stay awake (needs a comma before *then*).

1. ✓ Sally went home for a nap, then decided to stay awake.

2. ✓ When Sally went home, she took a nap before dinner (comma after introductory clause).

3. ✗ Going home was not her first choice, but once she made the decision she took a nap. (Needs a comma before *but* because it's a coordinating conjunction joining two independent clauses, and it needs one after *but* to offset the nonessential phrase that follows.)

3. ✓ Going home was not her first choice, but once she made the decision, she took a nap.

4. ✓ Bob went to the store and bought some ice cream and cake. (No comma is necessary.)

5. ✓ The dog that bit me, the German shepherd, is right over there. (Commas surround the nonessential phrase.)

Chapter Twenty-Four
ANSWERS TO QUIZ 2

Answers To Quiz Two

1. ✓ I went to the store and got some milk.
2. ✗ When I visited Italy I returned with limoncello. (It needs a comma after *Italy*.)
2. ✓ When I visited Italy, I returned with limoncello.
3. ✗ We vacationed in Europe, and bought a lot of clothes (no comma necessary).
3. ✓ We vacationed in Europe and bought a lot of clothes.
4. ✗ I went to Italy to see the sights, but also the people (no comma necessary).
4. ✓ I went to Italy to see the sights but also the people.
5. ✗ I took a train from Rome to Naples and while on the train, I saw Sofia Loren. (Comma is necessary after Naples because *and* is a coordinating conjunction connecting independent clauses, and commas enclose the nonessential phrase "while on the train.")
5. ✓ I took a train from Rome to Naples, and, while on the train, I saw Sofia Loren.

Chapter Twenty-Five
ANSWERS TO QUIZ 3

Answers To Quiz Three

1. ✗ I love Italian pastries such as, *cannoli*, *sfogliatelle*, and *pizzelle*. (The comma does *not* go after "such as"; it goes after *pastries*.)

1. ✓ I love Italian pastries, such as *cannoli*, *sfogliatelle*, and *pizzelle*.

✓ I love Italian food, such as ravioli, lasagna, and gnocchi.

✓ I love Italian food, such as ravioli, lasagna, and gnocchi, but not dishes that include seafood.

Chapter Twenty-Six
ANSWERS TO QUIZ 4

Answers To Quiz 4
- The dog was panting because it had just chased the mailman.
- You'll go to the beach when I say you can, young man.
- You can't go to the beach, and it's because I said so.
- Cell phones, which were a rarity even in the '90s, are now everywhere.
- Barbara earned fifty dollars for babysitting, but she spent it all on eyeliner and makeup.

Chapter Twenty-Seven
ANSWERS TO QUIZ 5

Answers To Quiz 5

☑ Bill turned to Jean. "That's what she told me. She said, 'Do it, or else,' and so I did it."

☑ We should stop and visit Maggie; she lives in Washington D.C.

☑ My kids loved the song "Who Let the Dogs Out?"

☑ Is the traffic bad in D.C.?

☑ Traffic is bad in D.C.!

Chapter Twenty-Eight
ANSWERS TO QUIZ 6

Answers To Quiz 6

- The onset of the clinical trial showed patients' tolerance for the new drug as "unacceptable"; the conclusion was quite different.

First, *patients* is plural, and it ends in *s*, so the apostrophe goes after it. Second, the semicolon goes *outside* the quotation marks because that's where semicolons go.

- The third chart from the left (see figure two) is the correct one.

Remember to place the punctuation in the sentence where it would go if the parentheses weren't there.

Chapter Twenty-Nine
ANSWERS TO QUIZ 7

Answers To Quiz 7.

☑ Bob and his dog *do* everything together. (Both of them do it—Bob *and* his dog.)

☑ My mom, as well as my dad, *is* going to the party. (It's my mom going to the party; she's just bringing Dad along with her.)

☑ *There's* a lot to do before we're done. (There *is a lot to do* . . .)

☑ He, my sister, and my dad *jog* every morning. (It's the three of them who *jog*, not just *he*.)

Chapter Thirty
ANSWERS TO QUIZ 8

Answers To Quiz 8

☑ He said he'd go to the theater (Will he?).
☑ "She said (at least, I think she said), 'Let's go to the beach.' "
☑ We saw a koala bear (have you ever seen one?) when we went to the zoo.

Remember, for punctuating around parentheses, say the sentence without the parenthetical expression, then punctuate it. So the last sentence would be punctuated as if it had been written:

- We saw a koala bear when we went to the zoo.

ACKNOWLEDGMENTS

It is with great honor that I give eternal gratitude to my wife and all four of my grandkids. They give me the inspiration to keep going.

ABOUT THE AUTHOR

Giacomo Giammatteo is the author of gritty crime dramas about murder, mystery, and family. He also writes non-fiction books including the No Mistakes Careers series, No Mistakes Publishing, No Mistakes Grammar, and No Mistakes Writing.

When Giacomo isn't writing, he's helping his wife take care of the animals on their sanctuary. At last count, they had forty-five animals—eleven dogs, a horse, six cats, and twenty-six pigs.

Oh, and one crazy—and very large—wild boar, who takes walks with Giacomo every day and also happens to be his best buddy.

nomistakespublishing.com
gg@giacomog.com

ALSO BY GIACOMO GIAMMATTEO

You can see all of my books here.
And you can buy them on the platform of your choice.

This brings up a thought: with more than eighty books out now, it is becoming difficult to try to update the list at the back of all of them. If you want to know what books I have out, use the link above, which takes you to my website, or download the latest copy of my GG recommended reading list, which is free.

Nonfiction

Careers

No Mistakes Resumes, Book I of No Mistakes Careers

No Mistakes Interviews, Book II of No Mistakes Careers

Grammar

Misused Words, No Mistakes Grammar, Volume I

Misused Words for Business, No Mistakes Grammar, Volume II

More Misused Words, No Mistakes Grammar, Volume III

Visual Grammar (this is a compilation of volumes I–III with a bit of new information added. It also includes pictures and is the world's first visual grammar book)

Misused Words and Then Some, No Mistakes Grammar, Volume V

Simply Put: The Plain English Grammar Guide

How to Capitalize Anything

More Grammar

No Mistakes Grammar Bites, Volume I, Lie, Lay, Laid, and It's and Its

No Mistakes Grammar Bites, Volume II, Good and Well, and Then and Than

No Mistakes Grammar Bites, Volume III, That, Which, and Who, and There Is and There Are

No Mistakes Grammar Bites, Volume IV, Affect and Effect, and Accept and Except

No Mistakes Grammar Bites, Volume V, You're and Your, and They're, There, and Their

No Mistakes Grammar Bites, Volume VI, Passed and Past, and Into, In To and In

No Mistakes Grammar Bites, Volume VII, Farther and Further, and Onto, On, and On To

No Mistakes Grammar Bites, Volume VIII, Anxious and Eager, and Different From and Different Than

No Mistakes Grammar Bites, Volume IX, A While and Awhile, and Envy and Jealousy

No Mistakes Grammar Bites, Volume X, Could've and Should've, and Irony and Coincidence

No Mistakes Grammar Bites, Volume XI, "Quotation Marks and How to Punctuate Them" and "Plurals of Compound Nouns"

No Mistakes Grammar Bites, Volume XII, "Latin Abbreviations"

No Mistakes Grammar Bites, Volume XIII, "Redundancies" and "Ax to Grind"

No Mistakes Grammar Bites Volume XIV, "Superlatives and How We Use them Wrong"

No Mistakes Grammar Bites Volume XV, "Shoo-in and Shoe-in" and "Horse Racing Sayings"

No Mistakes Grammar Bites Volume XVI, "Which and What" and "Since and Because"

No Mistakes Grammar Bites Volume XVII, "Hyphens, and When to Use Them" and "Em Dashes and En Dashes"

No Mistakes Grammar Bites Volume XVIII, "Words Difficult to Pronounce" and "Could Not Care Less"

No Mistakes Grammar Bites Volume XIX, "Punctuation" and "When You Don't Need the Word Personal"

No Mistakes Grammar Bites, Volume XX, "When Is Currently Needed?" And "Intervene and Interfere"

No Mistakes Grammar Bites, Volume XXI, "More Hyphen Questions" and Myself, Me, Themselves and Themselves."

No Mistakes Grammar Bites, Volume XXII, "Words You May Be Using Wrong, Part One"

No Mistakes Grammar Bites, Volume XXIII, "Words You May Be Using Wong, Part II"

No Mistakes Grammar Bites, Volume XXIV, "If and Whether," and "Incredible"

No Mistakes Grammar Bites, Volume XXV, "Use or Utilize" and "Dilemma"

No Mistakes Grammar Bites, Volume XXVI, "Alternate and Alternative" and "Plethora"

Writing

No Mistakes Writing, Volume I—Writing Shortcuts

No Mistakes Writing, Volume II—How to Write a Bestseller

No Mistakes Writing, Volume III—Editing Made Easy

No Mistakes Writing, Volume IV—Writing Rules for Writers Who Don't Like Rules (coming soon)

Publishing

How to Publish an eBook, No Mistakes Publishing, Volume I

How to Format an eBook, No Mistakes Publishing, Volume II

eBook Distribution, No Mistakes Publishing, Volume III

Print on Demand—Who to Use to Print Your Books, No Mistakes Publishing, Volume IV

Other Nonfiction

Uneducated

Whiskers and Bear—Volume I, Sanctuary Tales

A Collection of Animal Stories, Volume II, Sanctuary Tales

More Animal Stories, Volume III, Sanctuary Tales

Surviving a Stroke—Or Two

Life and Then Some

Fiction

Friendship & Honor Series:

Murder Takes Time

Murder Has Consequences

Murder Takes Patience

Murder Is Invisible

Murder Is a Promise

Murder Is Immaculate (coming soon)

Blood Flows South Series

A Bullet for Carlos: A Connie Gianelli Mystery

Finding Family, a Novella

A Bullet from Dominic

The Good Book

The Ranger

Redemption Series

Necessary Decisions: A Gino Cataldi Mystery

Old Wounds

Promises Kept, the Story of Number Two

Premeditated

The Ranger

Rules of Vengeance Series (Fantasy)

Light of Lights (the beginning, a novella)

A Promise of Vengeance

Undeniable Vengeance

Consummate Vengeance

Vengeance Is Mine (2019)

Note: The Light of Lights is a novella. It's about 100 pages long and sets the stage for the series. The other books in the series are between 650 and 850 pages long.

OTHER BOOKS

You can always see the current and coming-soon books on my website.

Fiction

***Memories for Sale* (mystery/sf)**

***The Joshua Citadel* (SF novella)**

Children's Books

No Mistakes Grammar for Kids, Volume I—Much and Many

No Mistakes Grammar for Kids, Volume II—Lie and Lay

No Mistakes Grammar for Kids, Volume III—Bring and Take

No Mistakes Grammar for Kids, Volume IV, "Would've, Should've" and "Your and You're"

No Mistakes Grammar for Kids, Volume V, "There, They're, and Their" and "To, Too, and Two"

Shinobi Goes to School—Life on the Farm for Kids, Volume I

Fiona Gets Caught, Life on the Farm for Kids, Volume II

Coco Gets a Donut, Life on the Farm for Kids, Volume III

Squeak Gets a Home, Life on the Farm for Kids, Volume IV

Biscotti Saves Punch, Life on the Farm for Kids, Volume V

The Adventures of Adalina, Volume I, Adalina and the Five Tiny Bears

Coming Soon

The Adventures of Adalina, Volume II, Adalina and the Underwater Bears

Get on the mailing list and you'll be sure to be notified of release dates and sales.

[Mailing list](#)

And don't forget to leave a review!

www.ingramcontent.com/pod-product-compliance
Lightning Source LLC
Chambersburg PA
CBHW060048230426
43661CB00004B/697